Patriot
Papers

One Citizen's Passion For A Greater America

Megan,

May the future ladies of America reflect your values.

With love,

Sal Terrusa

Patriot Papers
One Citizen's Passion For A Greater America

By
Sal Terrusa

AMERICAN PATRIOT PUBLICATIONS

TEXAS

Copyright © 2011 Sal Terrusa
All Rights Reserved

Published and Printed in the United States of America

No part of this book can be reproduced in any manner whatsoever without the written permission of the publisher except for brief quotations used in articles and reviews.

For more information:
e-mail: PatriotPapers@live.com
www.watchdogforcommonsense.net

ISBN 13:
978-0-9818391-9-6
ISBN 10:
0-9818391-9-3

Dedication

For my lovable and encouraging wife, Jo,
and a greater posterity for
David, Mitchell, Julie, Leslie, Chelsea and Tyler

AUTHOR'S NOTE

I have been asked the following question, "Why are you writing this book?"

After 81 years, I have witnessed unfortunate trends and changes in America. It is not a desirable transformation. The book entitled "Patriot Papers" was written by a man who loves his country and is willing to fight to preserve its goodness for his children and grandchildren.

Why do I love my country?

I love its people and, as a teenager, witnessed the greatest of generations pulling together during World War II to make the world a safer place.

I loved my patriotic dad, an Italian immigrant, who became a proud American citizen.

I loved watching my dad install an American flag in front of the family business on the 4th of July during WWII.

I loved the opportunity to realize a dream in becoming a teacher, football and baseball coach; and, an entrepreneur.

I loved the favorable chances it afforded my friends and relatives in realizing their dreams.

I loved its mixed history, good and bad, and the efforts to enhance its goodness. I love the patriotic resistance to any and all threats to our country and constitution.

I love the growth of tolerance in America toward minorities.

I love what America stands for—freedom and its willingness and ability to support all peoples of the world who are pursuing democratic forms of government. We need all the friends we can get in a hostile global environment. Tyranny is a constant threat to all freedom loving peoples.

I could go on. You shall be spared—I'm sure you catch the drift. Hell! I simply love my country.

Far too many members of congress have exhibited gross self-interest which has superseded duty. They have abandoned honor in failing to serve their fellow Americans. When a congress of the United States ignores three out of four Americans in regard to the recent passage of the healthcare plan, we have a tyranny in our midst. The country is trillions of dollars in debt which unfairly imposes upon future generations. The conservative and common sense frugality of federal spending no longer exists. We are heading towards devastating national economic ruin should we fail to react.

Our representatives in congress are misrepresenting the American people's will. Corrective action is in order.

All citizens are urged to learn about ideas that would restore our nation to even greater heights for the sake of our children and grandchildren. Submit your own ideas. Join movements that would lead to continued national security and prosperity. The most powerful of forces is the vote—exercise it at the polls.

As a former athletic coach and history teacher, I learned two significant lessons:

1. An athletic coach designs a course of action for fitness, skill and mental toughness. Success is created by drill, drill and more drill.

The result becomes physical excellence, discipline and a path to championship form.

2. A history teacher designs a lesson plan which does not omit the significant events of the past and/or facts which have determined our present course of action. Historic honesty is pursued by review, review and more review.

The result becomes intellectual integrity, an appreciation of the U.S. Constitutions and a path to assured patriotism.

American textbooks omit how our nation has been undermined by international bankers and corrupt politicians. Research, research and more research, available to the voters, is the key to accurate political decisions.

The correct assessment of history provides the basis for real solutions, not the impractical efforts of ineptly prepared politicians or a misinformed electorate.

Entitlements such as Social Security, Medicare and the Federal Department of Education are responsibilities of the states or the people, not the federal government. Duplicative federal bureaus of Energy, the Environmental Protection Agency, etc., etc. are bankrupting the United States Treasury. This book addresses these issues and far more.

An enlightened citizenry is the first step to redirecting our representatives on the path to the freedoms established by the Nation's Constitution.

Preface

THE CALL FOR COMMON SENSE

The chapters and articles on these pages, written by my dad, Sal Terrusa, address issues that every citizen should recognize as an important part of our quest to be a free and creative nation of individuals who, collectively, form the foundation of the national conscience, will and action.

There are universal and fundamental principles of Economics and Logic that function whether or not we believe in them, apply them or understand them. Just as the Natural Law of Gravity will function regardless of our actions or beliefs; these principals of Economics and Logic will function regardless of our efforts to change them.

Common Sense dictates that we work to embrace the reality of these principles in order to harness the power of truth. Once we understand and accept the laws that dictate results, we can master them.

We need a national political system that is designed to provide genuine opportunity for all its people.

It is only when we stop ignoring the truth and embrace reality that we will be able to influence the course of our lives, our country, our world.

In the United States of America, we need a solidly logical and realistic platform that citizens can rally around; a platform that respects our founders' design for a free nation where our leaders serve our citizens dutifully and with honor .

—Mitchell Eric Terrusa

CONTENTS

PART 1: A MORE SECURE AND PROSPEROUS AMERICA / 13

Introduction to Part 1 / 14
Chapter One / An American Manifesto / 18
Chapter Two / A Common Sense Platform / 28
Chapter Three / National Priorities / 33
Chapter Four / Energy: The Key to Survival / 43
Chapter Five / A Brief History of Banking and Taxation / 48
Chapter Six/ The Great Conspiracy: Abolish the Federal Reserve / 56
Chapter Seven / A New Tax System / 61
Chapter Eight / National Defense and the Common Welfare / 66
Chapter Nine / A National Service Plan for Volunteers / 68
Chapter Ten / Patriots vs. Parasites: A Case for a Term Limit / 72
Chapter Eleven / A Term Limit Amendment / 78
Chapter Twelve / Abolish the Federal Department of Education / 81
Chapter Thirteen / Congressional Benefits Reform / 85
Chapter Fourteen / Congressional Campaign Reform / 87
Chapter Fifteen / Congressional Protocol Reform / 90
Chapter Sixteen / Contract with America for the 21st Century / 92
Chapter Seventeen / Disturbing Facts About Obama and High Officials / 96
Chapter Eighteen / Social Security: A Ponzi Scheme Beyond Repair / 100

PART 2: AUTHOR'S LETTERS TO THE EDITORS / 103
 The Great American Betrayal / 105
 United We Stand…Divided We Fall / 108
 How to Win in Iraq and Afghanistan / 110
 A Thanksgiving Day for Enduring Freedom / 113
 Fair Play: An American Tradition / 115
 An Attack on the Second Amendment / 115
 The Federal Reserve / 122
 The Greatest President… Since Abe Lincoln / 126
 The Wisdom of Our Fathers / 133
 America: A World Class Paradigm in Crisis / 137
 Freedom: An American Dynamic / 142
 A Proposed Health Care Plan: Will Seniors
  Opt for Ice Floe? / 144
 A Greater America / 147
 People Power Politics and Energy / 150
 The Nation's Downfall: Over-Taxation / 154
 An Enlightened Civilization / 157
 Sarah Palin: 2012? / 160
 Is the Federal Reserve Necessary? / 162
 The Blow Out! / 165
 Who Are the Tea Party Followers? / 167
 Know Your Rights / 170
 A "Change" for the Better / 172
 "Where Law Ends, Tyranny Begins" / 175
 The Challenge of Capitalism / 177
 The Intolerable Acts of the 21st Century / 179
 A "Moratorium" on Earmarks!? / 181

PART 3: ARTICLES BY OTHERS / 185
 1938 Austria-Kitty Werthmann / 188
 The Federal Reserve-Enemy of America / 195

Patriots of the Revolution / 199
The 545 People-Charlie Reese / 201
Wayne Allyn Root-Overwhelming the System / 204
Financial Reform or Bust / 207

PART 4: CONCLUSIONS AND SOLUTIONS / 211
Power / 214
The General Welfare Clause / 215
A Simplistic Remedy for Distortions of the Constitution / 218
A Quick Fix for the Current Economy / 219
The Real Owners of the Federal Reserve / 220
How to Join a Tea Party / 222
Future Candidates for Public Office / 222
Constitutional Enactments and Statutes / 223
Candidates for Public Office Pledge / 225
The Rest of the Story / 226

Acknowledgements / 227
About the Author / 229

PART 1

INTRODUCTION to Part 1

A More Secure and Prosperous America

The promise of American freedom shall return to the United States when the tyranny of money is exposed and controlled. The power of money to influence and shape events is well-known.

The chapter entitled, "National Priorities" features the Federal Reserve as a priority for abolition. The chapters entitled, "A Brief History of Banking and Taxation" and "The Great Conspiracy: Abolish the Federal Reserve" further make the point for the absolute abolition of the Federal Reserve. The greatest threat to our liberty is the Federal Reserve - a private corporation of international bankers. Greed and corruption runs rampant with the alleged "Feds." The Federal Reserve has been exposed as the greatest menace to our freedoms. Fifty-one percent of the members of congress are needed at the next election to remove these banksters from our economic life. Executive Order 11110 may also be employed; don't miss this article. It is available on the Internet as well.

"Energy: The Key to Survival" is most significant in retaining our position as a world superpower. Every straight-thinking American desires peace over war. The nation's security relies on its military superiority to preserve the peace. Potential foes of the future would be more inclined to listen to reason should we discuss peace from a position of strength rather than weakness.

A new tax system must replace the income tax. The income tax is incredibly unfair, purposefully complicated, without limitation, and unnecessarily punitive. A new tax system would simplify the current 66,000 page income tax code.

The author prefers the Ad Valorum Tax (a property tax) on corporations and companies only. The individual would not pay a capitation tax or a tax of any kind. An acceptable alternative tax system would be a 6% tax of the Gross Domestic Product on corporations and companies only. Once again, no direct tax on the individual. Other systems are available for your scrutiny in the chapter on "A New Tax System". Citizens, the owners of the country, must never be intimidated by irrational, excessive taxation.

"When the people fear their government, there is tyranny; when the government fears the people, there is liberty."

— *Thomas Jefferson*

The chapter, "National Defense and the Common Welfare" proposes that the states rather than the federal government be primarily responsible for the Common Welfare. The Founders feared a central government that would compete in power with the status of the "Sovereign" states of the union. The Constitution was written to limit the powers of the central government to that which was inscribed in the Constitution. The General Welfare was reserved for the people or the states. Federal revenues would be transferred to the states to support the states' greater responsibility. The states would be financially responsible and, hopefully, more effective and responsive than a remote and wasteful federal government. Before the current recession, the state of California was the world's fifth largest economy. Presidents Kennedy and Reagan lowered taxes and removed waste from the federal government. Prosperity quickly followed. Overtaxation is the curse of the current administration and congress. We will know our financial destiny by December 31st 2010. Retaining the Bush tax cuts is insufficient; we must do more. Adopting the 1912 tax system is a start in the right direction. Cap and Trade is another way for the government to steal from your hard-earned salaries. It's all about the power to eventually reduce you to serfdom. If you trust the current government—your pockets will be emptied.

The security and prosperity of the nation is assured by military readiness and a plan for higher education. A plan for combat preparedness and educational benefits is addressed in the chapter, "A National Service Plan for Volunteers." Volunteer programs like the Peace Corps and AmeriCorps may qualify noncombatants for educational benefits as well.

Educational benefits for all volunteers would include the promotion of fields of endeavors such as math, science and technology. The nation's economic prosperity and security would be enhanced by these studies. A readiness for successful global competition would be forthcoming.

A Term Limit Amendment, with citizen-legislators rotating the duties of government, was an integral part of the Founders inspiration for a check and balance system. Career politicians, unfortunately, have neutralized the system. A term Limit would mitigate the power and corruption of elected officials. Twelve reasons for a Term Limit Amendment are presented in chapter ten.

Out of fear of a demanding federal government and the desire to retain their sovereignty, the states purposely limited the powers of the central government. The federal government could only perform those functions that were enumerated in the U.S Constitution. The states and or the people retained all other rights. President Madison ruled during his administration that the Common Welfare or entitlements were to be administered by the states or the people to avoid bankrupting the U.S. Treasury.

The federal government has abused many Amendments. An example is the improperly created Federal Department of Education. The chapter "Abolish the Federal Department of Education" explains why it is necessary. The people or the states have created changes or additions known as amendments to the constitution—27 amendments to date.

It is the people or the states that have the ultimate power to create or uncreate the constitution - not the federal government or its employees.

Our staggered system of the electoral process provides the opportunity for citizens to remove undesirable elected officials before they can do too much harm. The ballot can be less disrupting than the bullet.

The Second Amendment (the right to bear arms) protects the constitution and all of its amendments. "An Attack on the Second Amendment" in Part II is an article all Americans must read and understand.

Private commissions must be established to address matters inappropriate for the members of congress to resolve. Employers, not employees, have the right to determine salaries and benefits in the public as well as the private sector. Members of congress should not have the right to demand exclusivity in setting the salaries, pensions, healthcare and perks of any members of congress, present or future. The input of a commission made-up of private citizens in our political system would be more appropriate. Commissioners should also address unfair campaign funding and improving the protocol of the most failed congress in American history (an 89% disapproval rating in 2010).

Members of the commissions would be selected from the general public (much like jurors for a civil or criminal trial). Commissioners would remain incognito during their service to avoid attempts at bribery.

Chapter One

AN AMERICAN MANIFESTO

Three major issues have been identified as the primary causes of the nation's economic instability:

The Income Tax Amendment, the Federal Reserve Act and the absence of a Term Limit Amendment.

THE INCOME TAX

The Income Tax, also known as the 16th Amendment, was introduced in 1913. The IRS (the Internal Revenue Service) with armed tax collectors was created in the same year to ensure collections from the individual taxpayer. Prior to the income tax, only corporations and companies paid a federal ad valorem tax. In 1912, the ad valorem tax from all sources totaled 2.1% of the GDP (The Gross Domestic Product) of 37.4 billion dollars. 78 million dollars was the entire revenue for the federal budget in 1912.

The population was 94 million people at the time. In spite of inflation, less than one billion dollars for the federal budget was a remarkable feat even in those days.

In 1912, the individual did not pay a federal tax. It was unconstitutional for an individual to pay a capitation tax or individual income tax. The Founders understood the danger of taxing individuals. Individual taxation would give the federal government the power to tax an individual's income without restraint. The possibility of taking part or all of an individual's personal property would be at risk.

How true! Our forefathers were cerebral giants and honest compared to our current group of far too many corrupt and unprepared misfits. The lowest approval in Congressional history was recorded at 11% in 2010. A course for new incumbents is a must.

In 2010, with a population of 310 million Americans, The national budget is more than 1.2 trillion dollars and the GDP is estimated to be 14,601 (billions of dollars). Ten percent of 14,601 billions of dollars is 1.46 trillion dollars. My calculator cannot divide 1.46 trillion dollars by 310 million Americans— therefore, you do the math. If my calculations are correct, however, we have sufficient funds to pay off the 2010 budget with more than 200 billion dollars left over to pay down the national debt. If I am wrong—blame my math teacher or me for falling asleep in class. The current income tax of more than 66,000 pages and growing is unfair, inadequate, complex and punitive. The IRS can penalize you by assessing a late payment, charge interest, garnishee your wages, confiscate your property and incarcerate you for alleged fraud. Before 1913, none of these punitive actions were constitutionally possible for the individual.

Once again: "When the people fear its government, there is tyranny..."

—Thomas Jefferson

A return to corporations and companies paying the Ad Valorum Tax or a 6% tax based on the GDP (with no tax assessed on the individual) would lead to more than 40% take -home pay. The take-home pay would permit individual citizens to pay for their own retirement and healthcare plans. We would have thousands of fewer IRS agents. The government would be able to cut their budget by over 50%, eventually, without the obligation of Medicare, Social Security and irresponsible governmental discretionary spending—such as domestic earmarks and gifts to foreign nations, etc. What we definitely don't need is both an ad valorem and income tax—Just an ad valorem tax on corporations and companies only. An alternative Business Tax would be acceptable, as well.

The federal government has proven its inept financial responsibility—we are more than 14 trillion dollars in debt. Social Security and Medicare are financially unresolved due to the absolute mismanagement of our tax dollars. The federal government must limit its activities to national defense, international affairs and, possibly, making low-interest repayable loans to the states for long term projects from the U.S. Treasury. We must rid ourselves of the 14 trillion dollars national debt by paying the "feds" off with fiat money that our U.S. Treasury would print. President Abe Lincoln did it with "greenbacks" during the Civil War.

We may wish to consider fraud, conspiracy, racketeering and counterfeiting regarding the Federal Reserve System in a civil and criminal suit. Counterfeiting has been ongoing with banks for over two hundred years. The practice of fractional banking permits banks to print currency that is nine times more than actual deposits received by the bank. For example, had you deposited $1,000 dollars in any bank, the bank receiving the deposit would print paper currency equal to nine times the $1,000 dollar deposit or $9,000 dollars (currency not backed up by anything of value). Why is this not considered counterfeiting? If a private citizen would attempt this practice—that individual would serve hard time in prison. Let's nail the counterfeiting banksters. The statue of limitations does not apply since they are still doing it.

If nothing works in paying off the national debt, then "Drill baby, drill!" and use those funds to exclusively pay off the national debt. The profits received from the new oil would be independent of the national budget. The interest alone on the national debt is breaking the bank. If allowed to continue, our poor rating would elevate our rate of interest. We would be in the same economic conditions as the Greeks. Let's simplify taxation by making it fair, adequate, simple and less punitive.

THE FEDERAL RESERVE ACT

The Federal Reserve for the uninformed is a private corporation of international bankers. The Federal Reserve is a cartel or monopoly that in financial parlance would be considered a central bank. Central banks are larger banks. The central banks are in business to make profits for the bank and its mostly foreign shareholders. Its fiduciary duty is to its shareholders and not the American taxpayer. The American government is a customer of the Federal Reserve. The alleged "Feds" earns its excessive profits by making interest-bearing loans and assessing a million dollar security fee or bonus for these loans to an almost bankrupt United States government.

In 1913, the Federal Reserve Act usurped the constitutional powers of the U.S. Treasury (Article I, Section 8). The printing of currency and the establishment of interest rates plus the interest on loans currently goes to the Federal Reserve, not the U.S. Treasury.

How did this happen? It's a long story. Several Senators and foreign bankers colluded during the Christmas recess for congress in 1913. The fallacious name of the Federal Reserve System was adopted by the colluders. Americans did not trust central banks and were led to believe the "Feds" were an American bank. Wrong! "Reserve" was implied to mean gold or silver was in reserve. Wrong, again. There has never been an audit of the Federal Reserve, as yet. The word, "System" was selected because most Americans did not like banks, even in those days.

The Great Depression and the most recent recession have been attributed to the so-called Federal Reserve. By manipulating interest rates, economic crises are created allowing the "feds" to lend currency (paper money) and charge interest, thereby increasing their profits. The mortgage bubble, which is responsible for the current down turn, was due to the failure of the

Federal Reserve to monitor Freddie Mac and Fannie Mae and the smaller banks. The large financial institutions that were deemed "too large to fail" should have been properly regulated by the Federal Reserve—they were not. The bailouts should have been the responsibility of the central bank known as the Federal Reserve, not the U.S. Treasury. The greed of central banks impacts on all of our lives. Purposeful mismanagement by the Federal Reserve has enriched the "Feds" by collecting interest on the loans they had made to the American government. The Americans, in turn, would bail out the Federal Reserves string of smaller failing banks. The financial risk was transferred to the American taxpayer. The "Feds" should have assumed the financial risk as they were the culprits who created the recession.

An interesting co-incidence follows. Presidents Jefferson, Jackson, Lincoln, Garfield, McKinley and Kennedy opposed the central banks. Congressmen Lindbergh and McFadden condemned the Federal Reserve. Four presidents and one congressman died in office. Congressman McFadden, the most verbal opponent of the Federal Reserve, was assaulted three times by gun fire and twice by poisoning. The second poisoning cost him his life on October 3, 1936. President Jackson was assaulted twice by gunfire after he terminated the central bank and fired 700 federal workers. Both attempts at his life failed. He became the only president in U.S. history to leave office with a national debt amounting to zero.

The Federal Reserve makes contributions to politicians on both sides of the aisle for election and re-election campaigns. President Obama is not an exception and stated he believed fractional banking was a good idea. Fractional banking beats Al Capone and Chicago politics as if they were in the minor leagues of corrupt activity. Campaign funds are looked upon as barefaced bribes by most Americans.

Politicians are either complicit or ignorant of the Federal Reserve. In either situation, they are not deserving of political office. The public would benefit if newly arrived incumbents would be compelled to take a refresher course in economics and American history. We must reinstitute the U.S. Treasury to print our own currency and set interest rates that will support our economy—not destroy it.

Profits from loans made by the U.S. Treasury shall be deposited in our own Treasury and used for the interest of the American people. Foreign shareholders will just have to get along without us. The question arises: Do we want to surrender our financial destiny to self-serving foreign bankers or to the reinstituted U.S. Treasury? International bankers enslave – citizens must control their own financial destiny. A sign at a Tea Party rally read, "IT'S ABOUT FREEDOM STUPID!"

A TERM LIMIT AMENDMENT

Ninety–three percent of incumbents are re-elected. Incumbents have the benefit of name recognition, earmarks and campaign contributions from affluent sources. The sources include the Federal Reserve, medical, pharmaceutical, petroleum, legal, insurance, various other industries and national unions to name a few.

The longer an incumbent remains in office, the greater the opportunity for power and political corruption. A correlation exists for time served in public office: The longer the time, the greater the possibility for power, self interest and greed.

The 22nd Amendment was ratified on February 27, 1951 limiting the terms of the presidency to two four-year terms. Limiting the term of a president should act as model for other public offices.

The potential power and corruption should be limited to all public offices.

A single term of four to six years is recommended for all elected offices: The House of Representatives; the Senate and the Presidency. An exception may be the presidency of two four year terms.

Advantages for the electorate:

Our Founders believed in rotating citizen-legislators to avoid excessive power and corruption.

Limited public service time will be available for more citizens to take their turn in exercising patriotic duty with honor. Career politicians and/or parasites will be a thing of the past.

The long-term politician or career politician has had no urgency to get things done — he or she knew they would be re-elected 93% of the time.

Progress on issues cannot be delayed- since there will not be a second term.

Incumbents will soon live by the same laws they have made for their fellow American.

Salaries and benefits will be determined by a public commission.

There will be no need for spending time campaigning for funds for re-election—running for another public office can take place only after one year had expired at the end of the office holder's term. We do not want incumbents campaigning on the taxpayer's dime.

Supporting a successor will be incumbent upon the office holder if an agenda was not completed.

Party whips will have limited power over office holders if they choose not to run for another public office.

Americans will have the opportunity to prove there is no paucity of leadership in these former British colonies. The United States has definitely proven its exceptionalism.

Professional office holders, who are in demand, will still be able to share their talents in other public offices.

Fifty years in public office, however, doesn't leave much opportunity for the next generation or two to have a say in government. In a rapidly changing world, the old-timers are going to have to leave office much sooner. Accelerated technological advances will constantly demand new blood in Congress equal to the times.Candidates for Congress, the Senate or the Presidency must publicly and in writing declare they will present, promote and vote for the following three major federal issues:

1. The Ad Valorum tax is a property tax for corporations and companies only—not the individual. An alternative Business Tax would be acceptable, in lieu of the Ad Valorum Tax.

2. Repeal the Federal Reserve Act and re-institute the U.S. Treasury.

3. Enact a single term Limit of four to six years for all Public offices.

These significant issues will be followed by several other major national concerns: Read the Common Sense Platform and the rationale regarding all the issues identified in the planks. The rationale will be discovered in the following chapters and articles.

If you agree with the platform and, as a candidate, wish to have the support of like-minded Americans—take the pledge and submit your willingness to pursue all the planks of the Common Sense Platform to: A local Tea Party. Local support is the traditional way to public office. Contact www.teaparty.org Look for your state on the home page to find a local group.

How much do you know about the Federal Reserve? Take a four question true or false quiz:

1. Americans are under the control of the Federal Reserve System.

2. The Federal Reserve is a greater enemy than Iran, North Korea and al Qaeda combined.

3. The U.S. members of congress, the senate and the presidency have taken huge campaign funds from the Federal Reserve.

4. The Federal Reserve is not an American bank and is

owned by a majority of foreigners.

All the answers are true. See next page for verification.

Read chapters and articles on the Federal Reserve for further history of how these international banksters have taken over our government and pushed aside the U.S. constitution.

THE FEDERAL RESERVE = INTERNATIONAL COUNTERFEITERS?

If you still have doubts about foreigners controlling our financial destiny observe the names of the families who own the so-called Federal Reserve. The Federal Reserve is not what you may think. It is not an American bank but an international consortium made-up of a majority of foreign banks. The misleading named, Federal Reserve, originated in 1913 and favors the foreign families of these crafty international bankers and U.S. office holders seeking election or re-election. Information regarding international counterfeiting follows on the next page.

The Bank Owners of the Federal Reserve:
Rothschild Bank of London; Rothschild Bank of Berlin
Lazard Brothers of Paris
Israel Moses Seif Banks of Italy
Warburg Bank of Amsterdam
Warburg Bank of Hamburg
*Lehman Brothers of New York
Kuhn Loeb Bank of New York
Goldman, Sachs of New York
Chase Manhattan Bank of New York

(*Lehman Brothers of New York has failed and is no longer in business)

A BRIEF HISTORY: During the Great Depression, a central bank, fallaciously known as the Federal Reserve created the 1929 economic downfall of the United States. The Federal Reserve, a private corporation of international bankers, exploited its economic designs further by purchasing the control and means of propaganda-the media; not unlike what the Nazis did during the rise of the Third Reich.

The various means of mass-communication has been under the control of statist supported by the corrupt Federal Reserve for most of the 20th century and to the present day. The owners of the Federal Reserve are mostly foreigners who have manipulated Americans by way of the media: i.e., radio, newspapers, magazines, television and movies. Americans have been duped by these foreigners by controlling the content of most of the nation's major communication outlets.

Americans are being economically and systematically impoverished by foreigners who have prostituted the United States government with contributions to its highest officials. The "Feds" have had financial control of every penny earned by Americans since 1913. We have paid a heavy price due to the corruption of our officials by the Federal Reserve; and, will continue to do so until the Federal Reserve and its foreign owners are removed from our shores.

Fractional banking is a banking practice which involves the printing of currency without the backing of commodities of worth such as gold and silver. It is a form of counterfeiting. Citizens would go to prison for practicing this kind of counterfeiting. The bankers should not receive a pass – it is criminal activity. Fiat currency, without backing, is destroying our economy. The "Feds" have never been audited. World class counterfeiters, in any event, must be brought to justice.

Note: The Federal Reserve serves the profit and fiduciary interests of its bank and mostly foreign shareholders, respectively—it is not an American bank. The American taxpayer has been victimized by exploitation which includes paid-off political "stooges" of the U.S. Government.

Chapter Two
A COMMON SENSE PLATFORM
INTRODUCTION

BACKGROUND: The Tea Party movement involves millions of Americans of various political persuasions who have come together to challenge the political decisions of the administration and congress. Independents, Republicans and Democrats have joined forces to confront major issues upon which there is unequivocal agreement.

Issue # I - Constitutional limits have been ignored.
Issue #2 - Fiscal responsibility is out-of-control.
lssue #3 - Free markets and capitalism have been restrained.

Constitutional Limits: Article I, Section 8 of the Constitution provided for the U.S. Treasury to print our own currency and establish the rates of interest. A cartel of international bankers promoted the Federal Reserve Act in 1913. The Federal Reserve, a private corporation of mostly foreign bankers, usurped the constitutional function of the U.S. Treasury. Many of the Tea Party followers understand that we are more than 14 trillion dollars in national debt and desperately want to revoke the Federal Reserve Act of 1913. Our children and grandchildren shall be burdened with this unfair debt of the current generation.

The Founders included a term limit for the House of Representatives and the Senate as further means to strengthen the checks and balances of the Constitution. Enduring long-term legislators leads to excessive power, greed and corruption. Perpetuating the existence of career politicians violates the need to control the abuse of power and self-service.

There is nothing in the Constitution that permits the United States government to give our tax money away to anyone in this country or a foreign nation. Why give 400 million dollars to refugees in Turkey or any country for that matter when there is need at home for these funds? We have established charities for that purpose. We are giving money away that must be borrowed from The Federal Reserve and foreign countries. We have to repay the principal and interest. How foolish is that!?

The Congress of the United States should not have the right to determine their own salaries and benefits for themselves or future members of Congress. Members of congress should receive the same medical and pension plans as their constituents—no more or no less.

Financial Responsibility: The Federal Reserve thrives by foisting loans or fiat money upon the United States government. Our more than 14 trillion dollar national debt is an established fact of irresponsibility by the United States government. This incredible debt is in addition to trillions of dollars of unfunded liabilities for Social Security. Medicare is in danger of financial collapse within a few years. The new healthcare bill, if not repealed and replaced, will undoubtedly contribute to our financial catastrophe. Let us hope that mandatory medical payments are ruled unconstitutional.

The Federal Reserve is not the only player in undermining our financial stability. Successful lobbyists associated with affluent industries such as oil, banking, insurance, pharmaceuticals, medical and legal have influenced our lawmakers often to the disadvantage of less affluent Americans.

Politicians, under our electoral system, receive funds from these financial giants for re-elections. The career politician refers to these alleged campaign funds as contributions. Most Americans view these "contributions" as bare-faced bribes. Political parasites are still with us. Campaign reforms are in order.

In the 1940's, running for congress costs less than $1,500 dollars. Campaigning was managed by placing an A-shaped frame on the back of a used pick-up truck while the candidate used a loudspeaker to get his message across. In the year 2010, the average cost in running for a congressional seat averaged more than a million dollars. It seems only lawyers, doctors and well-to-do business men are able to afford running for office.

Free Markets and Capitalism: Capitalism has made the United States the greatest country in the world. Socialism has been tried and failed in the former Soviet Union, Great Britain and the European Union. China, a hybrid of Communist leadership and a free market economic system, is still under review. The Chinese question arises—shall a tyrannical government and a free market economy endure side-by-side?

The "Bailout" using tax payer funds is not pure capitalism. Bailing out the "too big to fail" insurance behemoth, AIG, banks and auto manufactures with taxpayer funds is contrary to a free market philosophy. A company that is too large to fail is a monopoly. A monopoly or cartel is against anti-trust laws. Regulators have failed — not the system. Regulators should have broken up the companies. The companies could have declared bankruptcy and reordered their businesses to compete successfully. Placing the American taxpayer at risk was unnecessary and foolish; a criminal theft of taxpayer money has occurred.

In Summary: Tea Party Americans believe in three common principles: Constitutional limitations; fiscal responsibility and free market capitalism. Specific social issues such as abortion, gay/lesbian rights, entitlements, earmarks and education are states' rights. These particular rights are not constitutionally within the federal domain. Double bureaucracies must be abolished, as well.

Most straight-thinking Americans can accept these three major issues. Enacting the necessary solutions shall be the challenge. An attempt to start the discussion follows with a platform and planks that may address the objectives for a more efficient, less wasteful, fairer, less intrusive, less expensive and smaller federal government.

You are invited to improve the platform and planks. *Please read the book prior to making changes.* You may better understand why the platform and planks have been arranged as follows. It may be safe to say prioritization was attempted. World events, of course, can change the priorities. Example: the oil spill in the Gulf of Mexico.

A COMMON SENSE PLATFORM

OBJECTIVE: Identifying candidates who will pledge support for the following major planks and values of the platform inspired by the Tea Party Movement. Candidate's political persuasion is a non-issue. Candidates must be willing to sign a contract for the 21stCentury to **present, promote and vote** for each of the issues* described below:

REFORMS
- Repeal the Federal Reserve Act of 1913
- Reinstitute the U.S. Treasury/ under Article 1 Section 8
- Repeal the Income Tax / the 16th Amendment
- Enact the Ad Valorum Tax or a 6% Business Tax on the GDP
- Enact a Balanced Budget Amendment/A zero debt plan
- Enact a Term Limit Amendment/a single term of 4 to 6 yrs.
    (Exception: two terms for a president.)

- Transfer General Welfare responsibility to the States
- Immigration reform/modify the 14th Amendment

STATUES
- Create a Commission for Congressional Benefits Reform
- Create a Commission for Congressional Campaign Reform
- Create a Commission for Congressional Protocol Reform
- Promote and accelerate all forms of energy
- Introduce a volunteer National Service Plan
- Abolish the Federal Department of Education
- Maintain Federal funds for Natural Disasters
- Establish a Research and Development fund
- Support elected officials only—no czars

If successful, ALL BENEFITS recommended by the new private commission would apply to current incumbents. All Commissions must be private. Only citizens, not elected officials, can become members of a Commission.

Replace Social Security and healthcare with congressional-style plans. Enacting the Ad Valorum Tax or a 6% Business Tax of the GDP will leave sufficient funds for individuals to afford privatization. Result: Reduced governmental financial control of our tax dollars and less waste.

Re: Healthcare
Government reform—yes.
Government financial take-over—no.

For a greater America—encourage all States to teach American history, traditions, customs, American English and the need for *unity* through the assimilation of uniquely American values and character. These core American values would contribute to the unification of the nation.

Chapter Three

NATIONAL PRIORITIES

Advancing freedoms of a great nation, nobly achieved by a blood-stained heritage, requires prioritizing the most compelling issues of the 21st century. We can disagree on the approach; we cannot ignore the urgency of resolve.

National security and a stable economy are the foremost considerations in resolving the nation's issues. A strong economy supports a superior military. The task to prioritize urgent national issues has been undertaken with a caveat—unpredictable events may alter the current priorities. A limited list of objectives is presented for prompt actions to resolve the nation's most pressing problems:

STOP ALL THE BAILOUTS... The poorly managed banks should have been allowed to fail. Why? The depositors were insured by the FDIC up to $100,000 for each account. It is now $250,000 per account. The depositors simply had to redeposit their insured money into a successful bank. An effective solution to save failing banks would be to monitor the "Regulators", the Federal Reserve — it would be far better to replace them. A double-check system to offset future failures is always a good idea.

THE FEDERAL RESERVE... Bailing out the failing banks preserved the regular customers of the Federal Reserve, a private corporation of international bankers, which regularly makes loans to smaller consumer banks. The Federal Reserve, a cartel, compelled the United States to accept fiat money in the form of interest bearing loans, thereby, shifting the lending risk to the United States Treasury. The U.S. government, in turn, loaned these funds to the smaller banks to protect the Federal Reserve's string of customers—the failing banks. The American taxpayer is holding the bag for assuming risky loans that were not in our best interest. The Federal Reserve, one of the world's greatest monopolistic money scammers, set up the American taxpayer to pay interest on loans that should have been given directly to the smaller banks—not as loans to the American government and burdening its taxpayers. The Federal Reserve profited by charging the U.S. interest on the loans to our government.

THE PRESIDENT OF THE FEDERAL RESERVE... Mr. Bernanke, the President of the Federal Reserve, failed to oversee his duty which led to the nation's greatest crises since the Great Depression. Mr. Bernanke, who was responsible for the financial breakdown, has been given credit for mitigating the financial crises that he had largely created by his inattention or design (i.e., a suspected collusion due to the bank's past history). Mr. Bernanke, unbelievably, was re-elected to another four year term as the head of the Federal Reserve. Mr. Bernanke and the Federal Reserve should have been dismissed and abolished, respectively.

The Senate failed to remove Mr. Bernanke whose fiduciary duty and primary responsibility is to increase profit for his foreign stockholders—not the U.S. taxpayer. An opportunity to return the printing of the U.S. currency and the regulation of interest rates was missed. Articled 1, section 8 of the constitution had not permited the printing of our currency or the regulation of interest rates to be contracted to outside financial institutions. The constitutional restoration of financial policy to the U.S. Treasury has been ignored since 1913. Incumbents have kept it that way out of ignorance or self-interest (they were paid off). This form of ignorance or corruption has not served the American people well.

An insurance company, AIG, was also saved with loans paid for by the American taxpayer. The Federal Reserve compelled our leaders to save a company that was "too big to fail." No single company should be so large that it could destroy a national economy. Anti-trust laws for banks and insurance companies, it appears, were non-existent or ignored. AIG should have been split into several independent companies to avoid the negative impact on our national economy. The so-called "Regulators" failed us, once again. The Federal Reserve's practice of indirect lending has plunged the U. S. taxpayer into even deeper debt. As of August, 2010 the national debt exceeds 13 trillion dollars; and, it is still climbing.

REPEAL THE FEDERAL RESERVE ACT OF 1913... The alleged "feds" are, once again, a private corporation of international bankers. Their shareholders are some of Europe's wealthiest families. Most Americans are surprised to learn The Federal Reserve is not an American bank. The fiduciary loyalty of the so-called Federal Reserve System is primarily and mostly to foreign shareholders—not the American taxpayer. The use of the word, "Federal," was fallaciously used to deceive the public in 1913 into believing that U.S. citizens were dealing with an American bank. The word, "Reserve," implied that their bank notes were backed up with "Reserves" of gold and silver. The word, "System," was used to avoid the word, "Bank". Americans have been suspicious of banks since the Revolutionary War. The Federal Reserve exists to increase profits for their mostly foreign shareholders—not the American taxpayer.

All of our recent Secretaries of the Treasury have been former members of the misleading international private corporation known to us as the "Federal Reserve." Mr. Geithner, the current Secretary of the Treasury, and the former president of the

New York Federal Reserve should be dismissed immediately.

A huge conflict of interest arises with the Federal Reserve—to whom will the current Secretary of the Treasury be loyal—to the American taxpayer or his former foreign shareholders?

EXECUTIVE ORDER 11110... President Kennedy signed Executive Order 11110 on June 4th, 1963 with the authority to basically strip the Federal Reserve Bank of its power to lend money to the United States. This executive order is still viable today and would effectively put the Federal Reserve Bank out of business. President Kennedy was assassinated on November 22, 1963. The Warren Commission was charged with the investigation of the assassination. The results were challenged by other investigative bodies. No president, to date, has exercised this still viable opportunity to rid the United States of these immoral money-mongers.

Executive Order 11110 is patiently awaiting a courageous Commander-in-Chief to enforce the order. No takers — so far.

A CIVIL SUIT... Further, the Federal Reserve Note is not real money according to several court decisions. Allowing the "Feds" to print our currency is contrary to our Founder's version of the constitution. Fraud and counterfeiting may be issues. It is past time to abolish the Federal Reserve and entertain criminal charges. Conspiracies to mislead American citizens have cost the taxpayer trillions of dollars—let's get it back legally by charging alleged fraud, counterfeiting and racketeering against the American people. These immoral and greedy international bankers must go—in any event. If the banks are allowed to continue alleged counterfeiting there is no hope for the world-wide economy.

AN ALTERNATIVE... Should a lawsuit fail, there may still be another possible way to reduce the national debt: Why not pay-off our debt to the Federal Reserve with fiat money printed by the U.S. Treasury? President Lincoln created fiat money, called "greenbacks", to support the civil war. The central banks, at the time, wanted to charge interest ranging between 24 % and 36%. You guessed it! President Lincoln told them what they could do with their money. The U.S. has assets or deposits of oil, gas and coal underground that would more than equal our national debt. Why not pay the Feds off with the same kind of fiat money they have loaned to us? Without an audit of the Federal Reserve—their fiat money may be equal to the monopoly money that can be purchased at TOYSRUS.

REPEAL THE 16TH AMENDMENT/THE INCOME TAX

Eliminate a punitive, unfair and complex tax system (over 66,000 pages). April 15th may become history with a new citizen-friendly tax system. Paying fines and interest on past due taxes, the garnishing of wages, the confiscation of property, incarceration for alleged fraud; and, the despicable threat to American financial freedom, leading to eventual serfdom, would fade away as a dark period of our past. The ability of excessive taxation to destroy lives and our economic capacity would become a bad memory. The decision to repeal the 16th Amendment and abolish or mitigate the IRS, as we know it, calls for a new tax system based on fairness, simplicity and adequate to meet our needs. A new tax system, in fact, which will meet all the basic needs of American citizens. The I.R.S., as we know it, would no longer threaten the individual taxpayer. Billions of dollars could be saved merely by no longer preparing complex tax returns. CPA's, accountants and tax attorneys—fear not—all the new businesses that will be created or forming will more than keep them busy during the former tax season.

Under a Fair Tax, corporations and companies, the new tax collectors, would be under the scrutiny of the U.S. Treasury. The individual pays all taxes due at the time of purchase and is not subject to tax inquiries. The Flat Tax and the Pre-1913 tax system may be possibilities, as well. The pre-1913 tax system deserves consideration. It is an ad valorium tax for corporations and businesses only — individuals did not pay a capitation tax. It was unconstitutional for individuals to pay an income tax because of tax code limitations.

ENACT THE FAIR TAX ... No taxes will be assessed until an individual or a family has retained sufficient funds to pay all of the individual's or families' basic needs. Basic needs include food, shelter, clothing, transportation, education, private healthcare and a private retirement plan. Take-home pay would dramatically increase with a Fair Tax which is a consumer tax, based on a percentage of the GDP (the Gross Domestic Product). Finally, the Fair Tax is a consumer tax, not a tax on income. If you don't spend, you don't pay the tax. Savings are encouraged through a private retirement plan. Unlike Social Security, any balance left in your account will go to your heirs. We need similar private pension and healthcare programs which are currently available to members of congress. A consumer tax would provide greater take-home pay of 35% to 45%. American taxpayers would have the ability to pay their own private healthcare and retirement plans as was possible in the 1970s. A pre-bate is included to offset the consumer tax due for the first $50,000 or a pre-determined average income.

ENACT THE FLAT TAX... The Flat Tax also features a pre-bate. The same percentage rate applies to all incomes. For example: At a 10% rate—if you earn $10,000 a year, you would pay $1,000 in taxes; if you earned $100,000 a year, you would pay $10,000 in taxes. There would be no other taxes due or deductions allowed. The rate does vary and is very popular in Europe. The rate variance may be from 8% to 28% in Europe.

GOVERNMENT SUBSIDIES... Government subsidies will not be needed for most Americans. The disabled are an exception. Unemployment benefits will still be available while retraining laborers for skilled jobs of the future that would allow a worker sufficient income to maintain his or her basic needs. A prebate would be given to each and every working citizen regardless of income. The established basic needs amount shall be determined by what middle income Americans earn. A smaller government would be less intrusive and optimal economic freedom would be returned to the American people who can best determine their own basic needs. American citizens would be free of governmental excesses.

ENACT THE PRE-1913 TAX SYSTEM...Corporations and companies paid the major share of federal taxes. Individuals did not pay a direct tax or a head tax. It was unconstitutional at the time. The federal government was able to survive very well with the additional assistance of other forms of taxation. I call these taxes the DIET. The **D** represents duties, the **I** stands for imposts, the **E** for excise and the **T** for tariffs. The DIET supplemented the federal revenues. The individual did not have to pay an income tax. Our trading partners, especially China and others are unfairly imposing tariffs against our exports. In the absence of a better plan, I would still opt for the Pre-1913 Tax System — an Ad Valorum tax (a property tax on corporations and companies only.) An alternative 6% Business Tax of the GDP in lieu of the Ad Valorum Tax would be acceptable.

Martin Luther King's dream – "Free, free at last" would extend to all Americans. The Pre-1913 Tax System optimizes individual freedom and financial opportunity.

PASS THE BALANCE BUDGET AMENDMENT and DEBT REDUCTION ACT... The government has failed miserably in preserving and protecting our national treasure. We are trillions of dollars in debt. Examples: Social Security and Medicare are catastrophic failures for future generations. A Balanced Budget Amendment would return sanity to the federal budget. A debt reduction plan to zero would eliminate the vast majority of tax dollars that go to pay interest only. The Balanced Budget Amendment failed by a single vote in 1994. We must try again and succeed this time.

The restraint on government spending and waste promotes a more prosperous and secure nation which would return the American promise for our children and grandchildren. A plan to reduce the national debt to zero to avoid the wasteful spending of our national treasure for interest is an imperative.

STOP THE PRACTICE OF GRANTS, GIFTS OR EARMARKS... Replace state grants, gifts and congressional earmarks with long-term loans and low interest rates. A congressional earmark by an incumbent to gain an advantage over a political opponent with taxpayer funds is unfair, wasteful of the nation's treasure and corrupt. There can be little or no equity in disbursing billions of dollars of taxpayer funds as grants, gifts or earmarks to the numerous congressional districts. States must expect to repay all loans, as well. Our empty Treasury helps no one except the world's greediest loan sharks—The Federal Reserve. The common sense way to maintain a balanced budget is for states and congressional districts to request a low-rate, long term loan to be repaid. Let's put a stop to draining the national treasury.

The financial future of the United States must remain with the U.S. treasury—not a cartel of excessively self-serving international bankers.

ENACT A SINGLE TERM LIMIT OF SIX YEARS... Unlimited terms lead to unlimited power and corruption. A term limit not only reduces corruption but frees the office holder to do his or her job rather than wasting time campaigning for re-election. Career politicians must be replaced by single-term office holders for the national interest. During the present healthcare confrontations among the *three* political parties, ask yourself this question: How would these incumbents vote on the healthcare proposals if a single-term limit would prevent them from seeking re-election? What would be in their self interest, if they were compelled to live by the same healthcare standards that applied to all Americans? Review the rationale of a dozen reasons for supporting a single- term limit. See the website at the end of this article for the single-term rationale.

We need patriots not parasites in public office.

A FINAL SUGGESTION: We owe trillions of dollars of unfunded liabilities to Social Security; Medicare is about to go broke; and, we owe China and other countries a bundle of money. China, India and third-world countries need the oil we have underground in the United States.

Let's allow our government to drill for oil in partnerships with private AMERICAN ENTREPENEURS and use the people's share of the profit to pay off our debts to foreign nations, thereby sparing future generations of Americans with an unfair financial burden. The oil we sell for profit to pay-off foreign loans would be independent of the annual budget. We may be able to do the same with the national debt. A return to pure capitalism requires that we sell the nation's partnerships to capable American capitalist after paying-off our foreign loans and national debt. Maintaining a strict balanced budget to avoid impure future capitalism demands the eternal vigilance of future generations.

Environmentalists—fear not—climate change has been evolving for a million or more years. We may still be able to use a modest decade or two, without significant harm, while returning the country to financial stability. In the interim, we are saving the lives of our troops by not purchasing oil from our Middle-East enemies (who would use their oil-profits to kill and maim our troops).

Drill baby drill! American energy independence now.

It is extremely irrational to place a moratorium on offshore drilling while foreign oil cartels will continue to drill. We must deprive our enemies of oil profits which are used to kill and maim our troops. Alternate fuels must be pursued at the same time.

A Republican form of government infers that people dictate their wishes to its representatives— not the other way around. Elections are held to determine who is listening.

Monitor the Watchdogs for Common Sense website for greater people power and avoid the nightmare of a socialistic, communistic or fascistic United States. Pass the facts on to your family and friends via the internet and encourage them to do the same. Enlightened Americans will keep our children and grandchildren free. The aforementioned issues must be addressed as top priorities. Equally important issues shall be posted regularly on the website listed below.

Website: *WatchdogsforCommonSense.net*

Chapter Four

ENERGY: THE KEY TO SURVIVAL

The American government has failed to resolve one the nation's most significant challenges—need for energy expansion. The first clue of the public's need for domestic energy arrived with an oil embargo by **OPEC** (Organization of Oil Producing Countries). The economy-destroying embargo occurred in the United States in 1973.

Today's young Americans did not witness the line-up of scores of vehicles waiting for their turn at the pumps for a limited supply of gas (a petroleum product). After kissing the royal behinds of the oil cartel pirates—oil began to flow, once again.

The need for a domestic supply of oil was ignored. The OPEC cartel or monopoly began to dictate the price of oil by increasing or decreasing the supply of the precious commodity— we call oil.

Oil is the current primary source of keeping all vehicles on the highway and all commercial airlines in the air. Electric or battery operated vehicles are sufficient for passenger vehicles but not eighteen wheelers, trains and commercial airliners. We will still need oil, possibly, for generations to come.

Environmentalists have been successful in preventing the United States, an oil rich nation, from drilling for oil. Their motives, I'm certain, were noble but unrealistic for the times. The world's leading scientists have given conflicting views of the climate and the effect of the carbon footprint. The scientists have predicted global warming, global cooling and, then, climate change (which appears to cover all the bases). Most scientists agree, we are experiencing climate change but not due to human activity.

The environmentalists and members of congress have agreed to advance towards alternative and cleaner fuels. It is my humble view that the reality of the present has been not fully factored in regards to the nation's priorities.

Some facts: $700 billion dollars was paid for Middle East oil in 2007. $500 billion dollars was paid for Middle East oil in 2008. It seems Americans were buying less fuel due to the high price of oil. The price of oil is still volatile as of 2010.

All Americans understand the need for alternative fuels and fuel-efficient vehicles. Many fuel-efficient vehicles have arrived. Not all Americans can afford these new marvels. The reality: it may take, at least, a generation for most Americans to convert to fuel-efficient or electric vehicles. In the interim, we will need fossil fuels to keep the older vehicles and trains running, the commercial airlines flying and the trains and eighteen-wheelers rolling.

The expansion of sufficient alternative energies may take several decades to develop as well as to implement the infrastructure. An international ban on the resulting carbon footprint is ludicrous at this point in world history. The growing economies of China, India, Russia, and Venezuela would not respect an international ban until they have attained military parity with the United States. More realism –there are over 180 third world countries that will need and demand the world's oil until their economies are sustainable. The U.S. would emulate the Lone Ranger if it fails to drill for oil. We cannot afford to allow our enemies and competition to outdrill us. The global population will explode in this century (the world population doubles every 40 years). More than 20 billion people will need cheap energy or oil.

What can the United States do to counter the rising military might of nations that would challenge us? How shall we explain to the environmentalist that a green planet is good but the security of the nation's people and military must take priority?

We can pray and hope that American inventiveness in creating a greater alternative energy supply will occur prior to an untimely catastrophic nuclear event impacting the entire planet. A ban on nuclear weapons that can be verified is a logical first step for the survival of human kind.

National security and the saving of civilian and military lives must take precedent over saving the planet. Saving the planet is a long term goal that must begin immediately. Saving the civilians and the troops is a more compelling goal and must take place even sooner.

Why drill for oil? Billions of dollars would return to the American economy and create jobs. Military preparedness would be enhanced.

Military lives would be saved by denying the countries in the Middle East the profits from the money we pay for their oil. Profits that some of these countries would use to kill and maim our troops. We have proven enemies in this part of the world.

The American production of oil on our land or seas could be sold to third world nations. Our foes would be denied market share, weakening our enemies' capacity for warfare.

The U.S. selling oil to these third world nations would place the U.S. in position to sell American surplus alternative energy and infrastructure as it becomes available.

Environmentalist must understand saving the planet is an admiral goal—it does not take precedence over diminishing our national security or placing the lives of our civilians and military in harms way.

Some positive news: Safe technology has advanced to the degree that would allow 30 to 40 oil lines originating from a single platform at sea. More oil means independence from the rest of the world, more jobs and money for the economy (without the additional eye sores).

Planes, trains and trucks will still need oil, possibly, for decades to come.

Did you know over 70 products must use petroleum for its manufacture.

The good news is that American ingenuity is capable of meeting the needs of the planet and the security of the nation without damaging either. Cap and Trade, however, is an added tax and will send American industry overseas. Cap and Trade is unrealistic and will definitely damage the economy. Larger world organizations, like the U.N., would love to be able to tax us into submission. A 1% tax would get their foot in the door—then we can look forward to undetermined amounts of taxation for a world government or entity which does not have our best interest at heart.

Write your Senators and Representatives before it's too late. A reminder: over-taxation equals under performance by the research and development sectors of our scientific community. Reducing taxes allows industry to compete among the 50 states. Universities, too, would join the search for alternative fuels. Federal efforts have failed to provide the nation's need for energy independence. Competitive enterprise reintroduces the proper role of the federal government to monitor and support the results rather than compete with the private sector.

An Urgent Update

The discovery of oil in Montana and the Dakotas as well as Colorado dwarfs the combined supply of oil in the rest of the world. Why is the find being kept secret? Drilling for deeper and deeper wells can be expensive. If we have the oil—we must go for it. Energy independence creates jobs and saves the lives of our military fighting overseas. Lives that are being lost due to the oil profits that our enemies use to kill our troopers.

Question: Are the environmentalists being paid-off by OPEC

and other other foreign oil-producing nations to continue their non-sensical pursuit of immediate climate change? The current oil-producing nations have benefited greatly without American competition. The fear implied by climate change has made an awful lot of people wealthy. What say you Mr. Gore, the Cap and Trade folks and other tax-interested members of the United Nations?

Chapter Five

A BRIEF HISTORY OF U.S. BANKING AND TAXES

Why is the financial health of the United States plagued by periods of wellness and hellness? The quick and simple answer is greed, corruption and power.

Alexander Hamilton, the first Secretary of the Treasury, chartered the first private bank in 1789. In 1811, President Jefferson refused to renew the charter of the private bank stating, *"I sincerely believe the banking institutions having the issuing power of money are more dangerous than standing armies..."*

In 1816, five years later, bankers persuaded Congress to establish the second private bank. President Jackson in 1836, ignoring the calls of Congress to restore the private bank charter (A.K.A. a central bank), commented: "The bold efforts the present bank had made to control the government are but premonitions of the fate that await the American people should they delude into a perpetuation of this institution or the establishment of another like it." President Jackson terminated 700 federal employees he believed were allied with the central bank.

It was the first and only time in the history of the United States when Americans were without national debt. Two failed attempts were made on President Jackson's life.

President Abraham Lincoln, during the civil war, approached the private banks (A.K.A. central bankers) for the purpose of obtaining loans to pay for the expenses of purchasing war materials and paying the troops. The central bankers, during the nation's time of need, wanted to charge from 24% to 36% in interest for these loans. President Lincoln bypassed these usurious banksters and had the U.S. Treasury print currency known as "greenbacks." After Lincoln's assassination, the greenbacks were eventually permitted to go out of circulation after the conclusion of the war. The central bankers reappeared during the Civil War Reconstruction phase. Presidents' Garfield, McKinley and Kennedy were assassinated shortly after announcing their intention to do away or negate the influence of the central banks including the Federal Reserve.

Question: What are the odds of coincidence taking place among the several assassinations after these presidents had announced their intentions to end or curtail the influence of these central bankers?

International bankers met secretly at Jekyll Island during the first part of the 20th century to plan the largest scam in financial history. The Federal Reserve Act of 1913 became law. President Wilson signed the Federal Reserve Act of 1913 dooming the nation to the economic control by international bankers.

The word "Federal" was purposely used to deceive the American people in believing the Federal Reserve was a U.S. Government entity. In essence, the Federal Reserve is a private corporation controlled by international bankers. Most Americans are bowled over when they realize for the first time, the Federal Reserve is not an American or U.S. bank.

Fact #1: A court case further verified the Federal Reserve's non-governmental status: A Mr. Lewis was injured by a Federal Reserve vehicle and sued the U.S. government. On April 17, 1982, the court ruled: "...that since the Federal Reserve System and its twelve branch banks are private corporations, the government (of the United States) could not be held responsible."

Fact #2: Unlike governmental agencies, the Federal Reserve

must pay for postage and taxes on their real properties.

The alleged Federal Reserve's primary allegiance and fiduciary duty is not to the people of the United States but to the international bankers and their mostly foreign shareholders—it was a bad business deal between an earlier United States government and the world's wealthiest bankers. This unholy alliance continues to this day.

This scam originated in 1913 and favors office holders seeking re-election and the families of the following crafty international bankers, the true owners of the Federal Reserve bank: Rothschild Bank of London; Rothschild Bank of Berlin; Lazard Brothers of Paris; Israel Moses Seif Banks of Italy; Warburg Bank of Amsterdam; Warburg Bank of Hamburg; Lehman Brothers of New York (which has since failed); Kuhn Loeb Bank of New York; Goldman, Sachs of New York; and Chase Manhattan Bank of New York.

Almost a century of economically controlling the American people was made possible through a quid pro quo arrangement i.e., The international bankers' relationship with the U.S. government could be described, in essence, as: Let us take over your banking needs and you will receive all the Federal Reserve Notes you must have towards keeping campaign promises for the folks back home (assuring re-election) and more.

Congressman Lindbergh (the father of the aviator) predicted after the passage of the Federal Reserve Act of 1913, "The new (Federal Reserve) law will create inflation whenever the trusts want a period of inflation...now if the trusts can get another period of inflation, they figure they can unload the stocks on the people at high prices during the excitement and then bring on a panic and buy them back at lower prices. The people may not know it immediately, but the day of reckoning is only a few years removed." Sixteen years later in 1929, as predicted by Lindbergh, came the worst financial depression in U.S. history–the Great Depression. President Wilson had signed the Federal Reserve

Act of 1913 dooming the nation to the economic control of international bankers.

Louis B. McFadden, Chairman, House Banking Committee stated in 1933, *"When the Federal Reserve Act was passed, the people of the United States did not perceive that a world banking system was being set up here. A super state controlled by international bankers and industrialists acting together to enslave the world for their own pleasure. Every effort has been made to conceal its powers but the truth is–the Fed has usurped the government."* The Congressman survived four attacks on his life, one by poisoning and three assaults by gunfire. Congressman McFadden was murdered by a second poisoning.

The money trusts or manipulators made great fortunes in the crash of 1929. These bankers, as a group, conspired to sell their stock investments at the same time. The next day, the falling stock prices caused a panic which worsened the crises. The stocks perceived as becoming worthless were purchased by the conspiratorial bankers when they had reached bargain basement prices. Against inside trading laws, the trusts conspired to sell high and repurchase these same stocks low.

President Kennedy signed Executive Order 11110 on June 4th, 1963 to prevent the Federal Reserve from lending money to United States government. President Kennedy was assassinated on November 22nd 1963. Vice-President Johnson, after he became president, failed to execute the executive order. Many Americans believe there may have been a cover up. The Executive Order 11110 is still viable today. We haven't had a courageous Commander-in-Chief, thus far, to activate the Executive Order.

Our present Secretary of the Treasury and past Secretaries of the Treasury have been former employees of the Federal Reserve. Employees of the Federal Reserve are responsible to the international bankers and their shareholders. How can these former employees of the Federal Reserve who made a profit for their bank and executed fiduciary duties to their mostly foreign stockholders serve the American taxpayer as well? It is not possible. A true conflict of interest exists. The current Secretary of the Treasury must be immediately terminated. The U.S Treasury, with a former member of the Federal Reserve acting as Secretary of the Treasury, is like having a fox guarding the proverbial hen house. A definite conflict of interest does not favor the American public. Why put our citizens at possible risk? Why not do what President Jackson did? President Jackson fired 700 federal employees who were aligned with the central bank, as you may recall.

I'm wondering if we have more than 700 employees, currently, whose allegiance is to the Federal Reserve and not the American people? How many are members of Congress?

A new tax plan would protect Americans from over-taxation. Greater take-home pay would cover the basics like food, shelter, clothing, transportation, education, pensions and medical care. Citizens would be able to pay for their own basic expenses. The out-of-control spending by the federal government, as a practice of the past, would be significantly challenged.

The 16th Amendment, the income tax, dramatically changed the tax code which was not in the best interest of the American people. The Federal government is now able to tax anything and everything albeit static or dynamic. The tax code is over 66,000 pages and growing.

Prior to the 16th Amendment an indirect tax was in place which meant only corporations or businesses could be taxed. It was contrary to the constitution to tax the individual on income directly. Many folks believe the 16th Amendment was never properly ratified. The I.R.S. has been challenged by some Americans successfully, we are told, and did not have to pay taxes. Others have tried to escape the tax collectors and failed. If you can afford an outstanding tax attorney–you, too, may be successful. The 16th Amendment, also known as the Income Tax, is often referred to by investigators as "the law that never was".

Tax Reforms such as the Fair Tax, the Flat tax or the pre-1913 tax system would free the American people from: tax penalties; interest on taxes due; garnishment of wages; confiscation of property and incarceration due to alleged fraud—April 15th would be just another day. A new tax plan would make the 16th amendment academic. Punitive fees would become a non-issue for most Americans. A farewell and good riddance to the nefarious Income Tax would be most welcome!

"The government should fear the people—not the other way around." —*Thomas Jefferson, paraphrased*

We need a fair, simplified and adequate new tax system now. The President could place into action an executive order creating a Blue Ribbon Commission made-up of trusted American citizens from a cross-section of society to evaluate the available tax choices. It may be possible to enact legislation providing for the study group to experiment. An opportunity to experiment with several types of tax systems at the same time may or may not be feasible. For example: Why not allow Alaskans to work with the Fair Tax in Alaska, the Hawaiians, the Flat Tax in Hawaii and the Ad Valorum Tax act as the tax code for the Puerto Ricans for a few years?

After the private commission evaluated the various systems – a recommendation for the most practical tax system selected would be made. Amendments would begin, at the same time of the executive order, allowing the new tax code selected to allow for its implementation, without wasting time for the usual legislative process, regardless of whatever tax code was selected at the end of the study. The American people should have the last word by the taking of a poll by a legitimate and certified poll taker to determine the choice of the majority. Representatives Beware! We, the citizens of the United States, need no further involvement of Representatives who have failed to respect the constitution of the United States.

To offset the horrendous national debt of more than 14 trillion dollars–why not allow the Federal Government and American oil companies to drill for the plentiful oil supply in the central areas of the United States, the Rockies and Alaska. Use the profits to pay down the national debt. The federal budget could be reduced by over 56% by using a consumer tax or the pre-1913 tax. Take-home pay would increase by more than 40%.

We need all the oil we can recover and not be intimidated by an unusual oil spill—it has been decades since the last spill. In 20 years or so, oil would be largely replaced by alternative fuels. In the interim, we must deny paying oil-producing countries, who don't like us, from using their profits to kill and maim our troops. Further, the 700 billion dollars we spend overseas for oil would better be spent in this country providing American jobs.

British Petroleum and all future oil companies must pay for all the economic disruptions by their neglect due to an oil spillage. Sabotage should be met with like consequences. Americans must overcome all challenges in drilling for oil and not be dissuaded. We are at war.

Why are so many Americans unaware of the international banksters? A possible reason: The money scammers own most of the newspapers, magazines, the airways, i.e., radio, T.V. and the movie studios. You are seeing and hearing only what they want you to see and hear. Informed and patriotic Americans are out there but you must seek them out.

A final thought—*"Let me issue and control a Nation's money, and I care not who writes its laws"* Meyer Rothschild (1743-1812). The character of Mr. Rothschild as expressed in the foregoing statement suggests values such as immorality, illegality, ruthlessness and arrogance. Such a man, by his own words and actions, in pursuit of unimaginable power, would make Attila the Hun appear to be an amateur. Why was Meyer Rothschild an unchallanged counterfeiter?

Do we really desire economic slave masters in our economic

system? If the greedy money masters of the current banking system can take your home and all of your earthly possessions—what do you plan to do about it?

We need newly elected officials who have the courage to confront and remove the international banksters who thrive on "legal larceny." The incoming Representatives must enact a new tax system as well. The election of November 2010 may determine the future of your sons and daughters—freedom or serfdom?

Chapter Six

THE GREAT CONSPIRACY: ABOLISH THE FEDERAL RESERVE

A QUOTE FOR THE AGES

"I believe that banking institutions are more dangerous to our liberties than standing armies. If the American people ever allow private banks to control the issue of their currency, first by inflation, then by deflation, the banks and corporations that will grow up around [the banks] will deprive the people of all property until their children wake up homeless on the continent their fathers conquered. The issuing power should be taken from the banks and restored to the people, to whom it properly belongs."

—Thomas Jefferson

The promise of liberties for all Americans has been compromised by a conspiratorial international banking system. Regaining the "promise" can be achieved by honoring a constitutional right to issue our own currency and an absolute vigilance over proper monetary policy. We must begin by terminating the Federal Reserve Bank (a private corporation) and returning the function of the alleged "Federal Reserve" to the United States Treasury. New standards for monetary policy must be established. A partial exposure of the Great Conspiracy follows:

The alleged "Federal Reserve" is a component of private international banks owned by the world's richest banking families, including members of several American families. The so-called "Feds"' primary allegiance is not to the people of the United States but to the international bankers—it was a bad business deal between an earlier United States government and the world's wealthiest bankers.

This scam originated in 1913 and favors the families of these crafty international bankers and office holders seeking re-election. The owners of the Federal Reserve Banks: Rothschild Bank of London; Rothschild Bank of Berlin; Lazard Brothers of Paris; Israel Moses Seif Banks of Italy; Warburg Bank of Amsterdam; Warburg Bank of Hamburg; Lehman Brothers of New York; (having since failed); Kuhn Loeb Bank of New York; Goldman, Sachs of New York; and Chase Manhattan Bank of New York.

Almost a century of ruling the American people was made possible through a quid pro quo arrangement i.e., The international bankers have pledged— Let us take over your banking needs and you will receive all the Federal Reserve Notes you must have towards keeping campaign promises for the folks back home (assuring re-election).

Without limits on borrowing from the alleged "Feds" or a balanced budget amendment to control our spending, we can now understand why we are trillions of dollars in debt. Guess who receives the interest on the loans perpetrated by your favorite career politicians? It's not the U.S.Treasury. The gall of the "Feds" is infinite; they pay no tax on the interest they gain from their loans to the U.S. government. A properly managed U.S. Treasury would eliminate the need for an international bank and collect the interest on its issuance of loans.

The alleged "Feds", even the name is a deception, have striven successfully toward astronomical economic gain and the pursuit of global power that would put Napoleon Bonaparte and Adolf Hitler to shame.

The "feds" are operating as a trust or conglomerate. As an exclusive monopoly, they have no competition in setting interest rates, while in the view of many, unconstitutionally issuing currency for the United States in the form of a Federal Reserve Note. The Federal Reserve Note, thus far, is not a valid currency via numerous court decisions. For example, "Checks, drafts, money orders and bank notes [Federal Reserve Notes] are not lawful money of the United States." (State vs. Nealan, 48 Ore. 155). The "Feds" have yet to be audited as of July, 2009. Printing our own currency would be necessary to avoid any future conspiracies or economic schemes (of any kind).

Further, the "Feds" control inflation or deflation at will, without constraints from any sector. Inflation is another form of taxation. The Federal Reserve creates currency by fiat (without accountability); and, gleefully, provides exorbitant loans to a nation already in heavy debt. These excessive loans expand that nation's debt and jeopardize its credit status and economic stability.

The people of the United States are definitely victims of the "Feds." Making loans to a heavily indebted nation at unsustainable interest rates impacts its citizens and creates an impossible circumstance to repay the new or old loans through excessive taxation. The inability to fully pay the interest on an annual basis implies the debt may never be retired. Hello!!!

Must we tolerate interminable debt for the greatest nation on the planet—leading to economic serfdom? Economists agree taxation on average American incomes exceeding 30% should be defined as servitude. I suspect the cumulative federal, state, county, and city taxes approaches 60% t0 70%. Many would call expropriating 70% of one's labor— absolute slavery.

Patrick Henry was unmistakable about the depth of his conviction; he did not say, "Give me liberty or give me forced labor." International conspirators must be confronted or we can expect to lose most of the fruits of our labors (including our homes and/or our businesses).

After the Great Depression, the perpetrators of global financial disaster were the only wealthy conspirators able to increase their ill-gotten riches. In the thirties and forties they purchased and controlled most of the media (newspapers and radio). T.V. became a part of their holdings in the fifties. Power is their game and they use the media to promote their self-interest. The Federal Reserve, an international corporation, must serve their shareholders first. The American taxpayer has become a victim of their incredible greed.

The So-called "Feds" are printing trillions of dollars towards the so-called Bailouts in the form of loans to the U.S government. Our grand kids won't be able to pay the interest owed on these bailout funds; trillions of dollars of the principal will still be a cross to bear. Pure capitalism allows failing businesses to go out of business to be succeeded by well-run businesses.

Saving failing banks protects the Federal Reserves own banks and its chain of smaller banks (their customers). The defunct Lehman Brothers of New York, one of their own, was too far gone to be saved. Why should the American taxpayer be involved in the bailouts? American depositors are insured up to $100,000 for each account (now up to $250,000).

The Federal Reserve manipulated the United States Treasury into providing loans to the failing banks. The Feds, then, collected the interest on these loans provided by the American taxpayer. The Feds also avoided the risk of making a direct loan to these failing banks. We, the taxpayers, were suckered, not only by the international bank, but by our own government. The international bank reaped the profit from the interest on the loans. The U.S. Treasury went into deeper debt.

We need to get rid of the Federal Reserve and the poorly operated smaller banks. The Constitution states in Article 1, Section 8 "To coin money—only the United States had the exclusive right to issue its own currency and to provide for the punishment of counterfeiting the securities and coin of the United States (the

Federal Reserve is a private corporation). Criminal infractions may be involved, including alleged fraud, counterfeiting and racketeering.

Terminating the "Federal Reserve" and returning the function of printing our currency to the United States Treasury would be constitutionally correct; and, a more responsible way to control our financial stability and destiny.

The current Secretary of the Treasury and former Secretaries of the Treasury have been employees of the Federal Reserve–a true conflict of interest. Whose interest will they serve—the people of the United States or the Federal Reserve and their shareholders?

The scheming international bankers, along with a few members of the United States Senate who created the Federal Reserve Act, also changed our tax system in 1913, as well. The 16th Amendment is a direct tax on the individual. The 16th Amendment gives the federal government the power to outrageously tax anything and everything without limitation. Prior to the 16th Amendment individuals did not pay an income tax— only corporations and companies paid taxes. What can we do about it? We must first repeal the ill-considered 16th Amendment. The Federal Reserve Act of 1913 must go, as well, to achieve control of our own currency and, frankly, our liberty.

Terminating the Federal Reserve by repealing The Federal Reserve Act of 1913 and the 16th Amendment is a primary course of action for economic sanity.

Let us not forget the words of the world's most infamous international banker: *"Let me issue and control a nation's money, and I care not who writes the laws"*

—Meyer Rothschild (1744–1812).

Google "The Enemies of the Federal Reserve" or the "History of the Federal Reserve" for more information on the exploitive conspiracy of the alleged "Federal Reserve." Let us never forget it is not Federal nor does it behave in the best interest of the United States.

Chapter Seven

A NEW TAX SYSTEM

Unlimited taxation leads to financial bondage, the rise of a permanent ruling class and the death of individual liberties.

The Income Tax became the law of the land in 1913 with the passage of the 16th amendment. It has become anachronistic with over 66,000 pages; it continues to grow in size and complexity. It is unfair, inadequate and complex. We need to abolish the income tax in favor of a fair, adequate and simpler tax system. Proposals will be forthcoming.

Our earliest leaders understood the power of unlimited taxation to enslave its citizens. The constitution, prior to 1913, limited the collection of taxes to corporations and businesses along with revenues collected from duties, imposts, excise taxes and tariffs. The capitation tax, the tax on individuals, was prohibited prior to 1913. The individual American did not pay any federal income tax prior to the arrival of the Income Tax in 1913.

The Federal Reserve is a private international cartel of bankers which has wreaked havoc with the American economy for almost a century, including the current financial crises; and, definitely, the Great Depression of 1929. It is not an American bank but a private corporation which exists for profit and the welfare of its mostly foreign share holders. There is empirical evidence that our public officials are in collusion with the so-called "Feds" or ignorant of their role; bad news, either way. The majority of American taxpayers are unwilling consumers of the loans the Feds impose on the U.S. Treasury. Article 1, section 8 of the federal constitution did not permit a private bank to usurp the powers reserved for the U.S. Treasury.

The foreign cartel has gleefully watched the national debt rise to over 13 trillion dollars with no containment in sight. Why not? The foreign cartel is collecting the interest on the loans to our government with fiat money. Without an audit of the Federal Reserve, their fiat money may be as valuable as Monopoly money at Toys R Us.

The barons of the international brotherhood of bankers and the signature of President Wilson allowed the Federal Reserve Act to become law. The punitive and "legal-theft" created by the Income Tax Amendment, arrived in the same year —1913.

The foreign cartel of bankers used subterfuge and fallacious words to win over the American public. The bankers of bilk used the title, "The Federal Reserve System". The word "Federal" was used to mislead the American public. The word, "Reserve" implied the Federal Reserve note was supported by commodities, such as gold and/or silver. The word, "System" substituted for the word, "bank", which the American people did not trust (even in those days).

Americans did quite well before the arrival of the so-called "Feds" and the Income Tax. We are presently the victims of a bloated federal government and an oppressive and unjust tax system. The tax was going to apply only to the "rich" and it began by being one percent of their income. The one percent fiasco did not last very long. How times have changed!

During WWII, the tax on defense industries was as high as 95% for American companies. We were at war and the excessive taking of profits during the spilling of American blood was frowned upon by fellow Americans. The incredible interest on war loans, however, served the Federal Reserve System well. The "Feds"—a non-American bank— were allowed to keep their profit without paying any tax on the interest of the loans charged to the United States. The Federal Reserve, a foreign corporation, was *exempt* from paying taxes on their war loan profits. In peace time, the progressive taxation of individuals increased continually without abatement. Due to wasteful and politically self-serving federal spending, the abusive and unrestrained Income tax is bringing American taxpayers to their financial knees. We have at least three choices to replace the present tax code. Let's start with the Fair Tax.

ENACT THE FAIR TAX ... No taxes will be assessed until an individual or a family has retained sufficient funds to pay all of the individual's or families' basic needs. Basic needs include food, shelter, clothing, transportation, education, private healthcare and a private retirement plan which is currently available to members of Congress, our employees. Take-home pay would dramatically increase with a Fair Tax which is a consumer tax, based on a percentage of the GDP (the Gross Domestic Product). Finally, the Fair Tax is a consumer tax, not a tax on income. If you don't spend, you don't pay the tax. Savings are encouraged through a private retirement plan. Unlike Social Security, any balance left in your account will go to your heirs. We need similar private pension and healthcare programs which are currently available to members of congress. A consumer tax would provide greater take-home pay of 35% to 45%. American taxpayers would have the ability to pay their own private healthcare and retirement plans as was possible in the 1970s (before government bloat became reality and the international banksters couldn't help pushing worthless fiat money— paper money) towards the American taxpayer.

The Fair Tax or a consumer tax on the GDP could replace the Income Tax. The Gross Domestic Product is predicted to reach 14 trillion dollars within a few years. Ten percent of the GDP would generate 1.4 trillion dollars of revenue for the U.S. Treasury—that would be over twice the annual budget of 2007. Further, all other taxes including FDIC and income taxes, etc. would be removed from American paychecks. Current tax obligations, such as the marriage penalty, the alternative minimum tax, capital gains and death taxes would be eliminated, as well. There is more—read the book: *The Fair Tax Book: Saying Goodbye to the Income Tax and the IRS* by Neal Boortz and John Linder (2006).

The increase in take-home pay would immediately impact the recession. The economy would explode with new spending and prosperity. Employment would soar. Future economical doubts would be abated. Presidents' Kennedy and Reagan returned prosperity by lowering all the tax rates during their stewardships in the White House. Do we have slow learners in the current administration or Socialists, bent upon destroying Capitalism – a system which made the U.S. the envy of the world?

ENACT THE FLAT TAX...The Flat Tax also features a prebate. The same percentage rate would apply to all incomes. For example: At a 10% rate—if you earn $10,000 a year, you would pay $1,000 in taxes; if you earned $100,000 a year, you would pay $10,000 in taxes. There would be no other taxes due or deductions allowed. The rate does vary and is very popular in Europe. The rate variance may be from 8% to 28% in Europe.

ENACT THE AD VALORUM TAX...The tax on corporations and companies was called an Ad Valorum tax. It is my first choice at the present time. Corporations and companies paid the major share of federal taxes. Individuals did not pay a direct tax or a capitation tax. It was unconstitutional at the time. The federal government was able to survive very well with the additional assistance of other forms of taxation. I call these taxes the DIET. The **D** represents Duties, the **I** for Imports or Imposts, the **E** for Excise and the **T** for Tariffs. The DIET supplemented federal revenues. *The individual did not pay an income tax.*

Our trading partners, especially China and others are unfairly imposing tariffs against our exports. In the absence of a better plan, I would opt for the Pre-1913 Tax System. A research group, hired by Glen Beck, said we have at least 50% waste among all the federal bureaucracies. Let's check it out with a private commission similar to President Reagan's Grace Commission.

The greatest benefits of a new tax code: We would not be saddled with the punitive Income Tax code, e.g., late penalties, interest, the garnishment of wages and the confiscation of property. Further, incarceration for fraud or alleged fraud would apply only to the tax collectors—corporations and businesses—not the individuals.

We must break the shackles of the alleged Federal Reserve for our economic freedom. I.R.S. agents would not need as many guns if "legal larceny" was under control. Lest we forget...Governments should fear the people–not the other way around. The people are in charge — not politicians or their foreign or domestic lobbyists.

Chapter Eight

NATIONAL DEFENSE AND THE COMMON WELFARE

The federal government has duplicated virtually every department that each state government already has in place. The exceptions, of course, are the Department of Defense, the State Department, Homeland Security, Immigration and departments associated with international or interstate affairs.

The largest states of the union have economies which are greater than many of the world's independent nations. California, for example, is the world's 8th largest economy. California and several other states are capable of nationhood and /or independent action. National defense of the nation is enhanced, however, by the addition of these larger states to the union. States of the union, in any event, do not need double bureaucracies. Do we really need numerous and highly expensive federal buildings in every state of the union? Duplication is extremely wasteful and the American taxpayer should demand the removal of extraordinary waste wherever it occurs. Failure to redeem wasteful spending denies the American taxpayer funds that every individual or family could better use for themselves. It should be considered a reckless theft of one's labors.

The national defense is the primary role of the federal government. Federal departments, appropriate to the functioning of a nation, must obviously be retained. Funds should be set aside, as well, in the federal treasury for: Natural disasters; Economic downturns; Loans for the states (long-term with low rates of interest); Loans for Allies and friendly nations. Loans available only if funds do not exceed the national budget.

The common welfare, especially as it relates to social and/or entitlement programs would be best served as a state responsibility. Federal revenues for Social Security and Medicare should be paid directly to the States with shortfalls complemented by the Federal government (until the programs are phased out). The programs available to members of congress should be made available to the next generation of Americans.

Each state has social problems uniquely inherent to that particular state or region. The state or local authority is usually in the supreme position to resolve its own peculiar issues. The federal government's involvement should take place only in a supplementary way when necessary, if at all. Example: a request for a low interest and long-term loan for a state or interstate project.

For effective governance we must constantly remind our elected officials that National Defense and international affairs are primarily federal roles. The Common Welfare is better suited as a primary role for the states and territories, as intended by the Founders.

A Balanced Budget Amendment, with a limit based on a percentage of the Gross National Product, would protect future generations from the financial abuses of the current generation. It would be helpful to reduce the national debt, as soon as possible, and save unnecessary billions of dollars expended on the interest before it becomes trillions. Interest payments make the international and local bankers wealthier and the poor, poorer.

National budgeters would do well to emulate responsible American families who actually never spend more than they make and save for the rainy day scenario.

Chapter Nine

A NATIONAL SERVICE PLAN FOR VOLUNTEERS

The President and the Congress would serve our nation and its veterans well by enacting legislation to provide a National Service Plan for volunteers.

American citizens would have the opportunity to demonstrate meaningful gratitude for our veterans; a brighter future for their service and a greater contribution toward the nation's continued economic prosperity and security. The National Service Plan for Volunteers must be enacted as soon as practical.

BACKGROUND: The liberties we all enjoy secured by the lives and limbs of our fellow Americans, past and present, face continued challenges in an unpredictable and dangerous world. The preservation of our freedom is dependent upon all Americans accepting the duties of citizenship, and capable Americans sharing the risks of combat. A declaration of war is the call for every citizen to support the troops and their leaders. Unity of action, until the cessation of hostilities, assures a higher degree of success. Division among our fellow Americans, during wartime, only serves the enemy.

The greater security of a nation is founded upon a prosperous economy willing to support a military unmatched by potential foes in the present or the future. An all volunteer plan for national service with educational benefits is a major step in that direction. The G.I. bill of WWII created an enlightened society contributing to the greatest economy and military the world had ever known.

Military training, with the inducement of educational benefits, contributes to the strong defense of the country and a prosperous economy; all necessary funds for the National Service Plan should be derived from the defense budget. The constitutional and primary role of the federal government is the defense of the United States. The Common Welfare responsibility of the federal government should be limited to national catastrophes; local and state governments should bear the greater responsibility. The savings from streamlining the federal government would not only support defense spending but would lead to financial stability—double bureaucracies would be eliminated. For example, we have 50 Departments of Education—the federal Department of Education is superfluous, interferes with the ongoing competition among the states and violates the 10th Amendment. It makes sense to reduce taxes to the federal government and shift revenues to the states—waste closer to home is much easier to monitor.

A PLAN FOR NATIONAL SERVICE: A recommendation for the long-term security of the nation and economic prosperity is to provide eligible high school graduates, both men and women, the opportunity to serve their country for 18-24 months as a duty of citizenship with minimal pay. All volunteers would train for four months in basic military skills and an additional two months in a specialized field (military or civil). The remaining 12-18 months may be in the U.S. Military, National Guard, the Coast Guard and U.S. Border Patrol or as Federal firefighters. Young Americans, after basic training, may choose to serve in non-combative organizations i.e., the Peace Corps, AmeriCorps, or The National Parks system. Skilled young Americans, serving overseas, could build friendships and future allies. Diplomatic ties with future allies enhance the peace process.

THE BENEFITS: two years of college tuition, books and reasonable living expenses from a grateful nation for completing basic, specialized training and service. Encourage careers in math, science and engineering with added inducements–a boon to the nation's future.

A four-year scholarship would be awarded for those who elect the military or other high risk services for the remaining 12-18 months. All will become active or inactive reservists for eight years and standby for four years. Trained young men and women would be prepared to defend our nation, if necessary. With the availability of greater reserves, the rotation of our troops would lower the risk levels for overly stressed troops and their families. Multiple tours of duty may become history; military suicides and fratricides due to the psychological shock of sustained warfare, would be minimized. An accepted volunteer, during enlistment, may designate a person to receive his or her educational benefits in the event of death or disability. Young Americans, enjoying their liberties, would share the challenges and risks maintaining those freedoms. College undergrads and graduates may also apply; benefits would apply for post-graduate work.

An all volunteer military, as provided by National Service Program, may be sufficient to prevent military adventurisms by potential foes. The best way to maintain the peace is to be well prepared for war or negotiations; and, to be victorious in the event a state of war is unavoidable. In a full- blown war, a military draft would be a last resort.

A National Service program with higher educational opportunities shall keep the United States secure and prosperous. Until a "peace pill" is created and hostile tyrants are willing to be sedated, we need to maintain a military second to none.

RECOMMENDED STANDARDS: Achievement and success criteria must be established.

For example: A "C" average or above must be maintained; a minimum of 12 units per semester must be taken; 20 hours of part-time work is the maximum allowed for a full-time student. Re: A student's lack of performance consequences—a warning, professional tutoring, probation, aptitude testing and/or counseling for a new direction.

Chapter Ten

PATRIOTS vs. PARASITES
The Case for a Term Limit

Background: The creators of the Constitution were learned and experienced in the affairs and nature of men. Our early leaders knew positions of power may be exercised for good or evil. To protect the people from an abuse of power by members of Congress, which appeared to be foremost in their minds, they limited a senator to a six-year term and a representative to a two-year term. Our founders intended that the new republic be governed by citizen-legislators who would accept the duty and honors bestowed upon them; and then, after serving their term, return to private life and live by the same laws they had enacted for their fellow citizens. They viewed their service as a patriotic duty—not as parasites entertaining a lifetime of public service and extraordinary benefits.

Our mostly agrarian forefathers, who were the first members of Congress, strongly desired to return to their farms before foreclosure became a reality— congressional pay was extremely low. This was equally true of the professionals and merchants as it related to their practices and businesses. In spite of the honor and duty bestowed upon these early lawmakers by their fellows, there was a distinct aversion to prolonged public service, because personal economic survival was at stake.

Let's contrast their concept of limited service to today's politicians. Most modern-day politicians seek a lifetime of service with salaries, perks and pensions that their fellow Americans could never achieve in a lifespan of labor (skilled or otherwise). Career politicians have become suspect in furthering their own self-interest over the best interests of their constituents. We have more than a few public officials behind bars; nevertheless, the parasitic age has arrived.

Many career politicians would argue, however, that experience gathered from longer service makes them invaluable in their public service. They insist on the validity of their claim while the highest office of the land, the presidency, is limited to no more than two 4-year terms. If the principle of restricting the power and influence of a president is recognized, why are senators and representatives exempt? Hypocrisy!

Power, prestige, position, or personal aggrandizement, perhaps, plays a part in making it impossible to pass up a parasitic lifestyle. The original political plan has been broken and replaced by a systemic ruling class. The ruling plan for the early American Republic was designed to include citizen representatives and senators on a share-the-power basis. All capable citizens had a duty and a responsibility to participate in self-governance. The periodic rotation of citizen leaders was intended to counter the formation of an excessively powerful and permanent ruling class—the European model of elitism was to be avoided.

We now have a well-paid ruling class that has ignored the original term limits. We have re-learned what our forefathers already knew: Unlimited terms lead to absolute power. Absolute power leads to absolute corruption (a paraphrase inspired by John Acton et al.). If a practical term limit must be reimposed, it should be no more than six years for any elected office. The excessive influence of money allows incumbents to remain in office for decades, a factor that has compromised the checks and balances of current-day government. More than 90% of incumbents are re-elected. A term limit of four years or less may be too brief to achieve the expertise and experience necessary for success in an increasingly more complex society. A term of more than six years may engender the power to aggrandize one's self-interest, leading to continued corruption and greed.

The American contempt for a nefarious ruling class is well known. The freedoms secured by self-government must be the bulwark against tyrannies such as communism, fascism or socialism.

The general election should be held in September instead of November. This would give candidates-elect four months to learn the standards of congressional protocol and parliamentary procedure. The extra time would also give the candidates-elect more time to be briefed thoroughly on the pros and cons of the current issues as well as historically significant legislation.

Public financing would also level the playing field for underfunded campaigns competing against wealthier campaigns (which tend to mute the cry of abusing the First Amendment- the right of free speech). A candidate's income should not be a prime factor for electing capable candidates.

Why a term limit? A term limit is a significant tool contributing to the checks and balances of our political system. A term limit invites greater participation by more Americans and the termination of a permanent ruling class. A term limit counters, to a degree, the overwhelming influence of special interests and their deep pockets.

With a term limit and true campaign reform we may expect, in the future, the resolve of most of our national issues. The failure of the federal government to perform, in the optimum interest of the American people, is disgraceful and must be challenged on many issues in addition to creating a term limit. Incumbents currently spend much of their time daily campaigning or raising funds for the next election during the period they should be doing the people's business. Under the new amendment, campaigning or fund raising will be disallowed during the time they are in office; incumbents would now spend a full six years of their time doing the people's business. Government waste by incumbents will cease. They will not be campaigning on our dime for the next election.

A Term Limit Amendment: An amendment to the Constitution would be necessary to limit a term of four to six years to an elected position. Public offices would include one term only for a Senator or a member of the House of Representatives. An incumbent may not run for the same public office but once. After a year had expired, an incumbent may campaign for other public offices (never the same public office).

Limited power leads to limited corruption.

Millions of dollars are currently expended to be re-elected, which limits access to public office to candidates with greater monetary resources. A potential candidate with the IQ of an Einstein and the salary of a professor could not reasonably expect to compete for public office. What a waste of talent and human resources!

Rationale: A term limit of six years for all elected officials would be in keeping with a more responsive and less entrenched ruling class.

Incumbents would focus on the issues at hand and persuading their colleagues of their merits, knowing they would have only a six-year window to accomplish their objectives—not 30 or 40 years as a career politician. After leaving office, supporting a like-minded successor would be a way to continue the advance of their political views. Incumbents would achieve independence of thought, without fear of party punishment by withholding campaign funds for the next election; there would not be a second or third term—a single term only. Public financing may be available in the future. Public financing of candidates who qualify for the general election further mitigates the burden of raising campaign funds.

All qualified candidates should have equal access to public

media during the campaign season.

The power of the political "whip" traditionally used for "block voting" on an issue would be diminished—the practice of withholding campaign funds for re-election would no longer be a serious threat. The incumbent would be free to act out of conscience and wisdom rather the political pressure applied by the party's whip.

Incumbents would realize they will be returned to private life after four to six years and must live by the same rules they made for their fellow Americans.

More Americans would have an opportunity to serve, contributing diverse ideas or issues of their own. Rapid technological advances would require "new blood" more often.

A "lifetime" ruling class is un-American and contrary to our forefathers' intent of capable American citizens sharing and rotating the duties of public office—not a permanent "ruling class" remaining in office until the Chicago Cubs win the pennant.

Long-term, highly salaried office holders are not experiencing the "pain" of fellow Americans during a recession or depression. Commiseration is difficult when the employee is economically more stable than the employer. We, the people, lend our power to our elected representatives. We, the people, can withdraw that power at the very next election. A Term Limit Amendment enhances the process.

Corruption such as financial fraud or recompense of any kind would result in prosecution involving fines and/or imprisonment. Parasites or opportunists will be compelled to seek employment elsewhere.

Public campaigning will be limited to 12 weeks (the British allow only six weeks). The media may suffer a drought and will be hard pressed to find newsworthy stories. Media comedians may experience a drop in the ratings when political humor dries up after twelve weeks but so be it.

There is no paucity of capable citizens to take on congressional duties or make a run for the White House. If a "good man" or "women" is term limited—he or she can run for another public office after a year has passed. We don't want office holders campaigning for the next office on our dime. If an elected official shows promise—encourage such talent to be shared by serving in other governmental offices such as the mayorship, senate, a governorship, or the presidency, etc.

A certificate of merit and gratitude would be entitled "Patriot" and awarded to a successful incumbent for honorable service—much like and honorable discharge from the military. Opportunists or parasites seeking a lifetime of plucking the public purse and other after-office perks may become individuals of historical insignificance.

A public commission, not members of congress, should determine the benefits of elected officials; but, that is another story.

It is past time for more citizens to participate at all levels of government. Become involved. How say you? All or any proposals are subject to scrutiny and counterproposals.

Chapter Eleven

A TERM LIMIT AMENDMENT

The founders of the United States and authors of the Constitution understood the nature of man and the potential abuses of power by self-serving politicians. Checks and balances, including a term limit, were established by the founders to counteract the influences of malfeasance in office. Career or multiple–term politicians enjoy the prestige, power, position and benefits of retaining public office. Unlimited terms in office, unfortunately, provide the occasions for unlimited power and corruption.

A true patriot understands the dangers of corruption associated with multiple terms and would not run for re-election (if only to set an example). A single Term Limit Amendment of four to six years honors the wisdom of our founders. It is my personal view that all elected officials should not serve more than one four to six year term. The founders' concept of rotating citizen-legislators to govern fellow citizens and mitigate corruption has been ignored.

Current long-term office holders have neutralized the intent of the checks and balance system. Most career politicians have been spoiled rotten, ignored constitutional restraints and need to be replaced at the very next elections. A dozen reasons exist for passing a Term limit Amendment—refer to: *watchdogsforcommonsense.net*

In the 2010 elections, and all elections thereafter, Americans must elect candidates who will pledge to present, promote and vote for a single Term Limit Amendment of four to six years.

The recall election and or impeachment procedure will remain viable options for bad governance.

Long–term or current career politicians must yield to the single term patriot to minimize the opportunities for continuing corruption and self-serving reputations. People power requires that all current incumbents must be replaced every election cycle.

We must instruct a failed congress (with the lowest approval rating in American history) that the people are the ultimate deciders of their own destiny. Sending the message of starting over with a new uncontaminated congress reminds future politicians that the people are still and always will be in charge of their Republic and its representatives.

It matters not a new candidate's political persuasion – only that the interest of the American people comes before party loyalty. The failure of congress to listen to the clear concerns of fellow citizens is unacceptable. A history of a candidate's unfailing character is our primary assurance.

We have bribery running rampant in the current healthcare bill. Trading senatorial votes for cash to pass the healthcare bill is repugnant to straight thinking Americans. A hundred million for the Cornhusker state and three hundred million for the "second" Louisiana Purchase, at the expense of the other 48 states of the union, have embarrassed the fair-minded citizens of these two states.

We fought a Revolutionary War to rid ourselves of absolute rulers. The undeniable power and corruption associated with decades of holding public office has become shockingly transparent and outrageous in the recent attempt to pass an unpopular and unclear healthcare bill (with over 2000 pages and unread by most members of congress). Moving towards an autocratic government and behind-closed-doors shady deals is un-American. The federal government has exceeded its power and violated the people's trust.

The choice is clear—what do Americans want— limited term

patriots, serving for duty and honor, without great material expectations or career politicians who enjoy excessive power, unwarranted prestige and the dependency on a parasitic life-style? One Revolutionary War should have been sufficient.

Become politically involved. Demand candidates pledge or vow to present, promote and vote for your issues.

American power for real change, fortunately, is the vote. Use your vote as a weapon.

Chapter Twelve

ABOLISH THE FEDERAL DEPARTMENT OF EDUCATION

An unconstitutional Department of Education (D.O.E) is dominating freedom-loving Americans. Common sense in the 21st century must be the catalyst for an immediate counteraction to this catastrophic threat to our Union.

The federal government imposing its standards such as "No Child Left Behind" and so-called "entitlements" is unconstitutional. The 10th Amendment gives the states or the people the right to any and all matters not specified in the Constitution. Education is a state and peoples right; the Feds are failing to recognize their limits. A national D.O.E restricts American freedom to create and innovate. An unconstitutional Department of Education and Congress have failed to acknowledge the usual upward surge generated by educational competition among the states.

The solution for quality education lies in the power of the states to compete and compare. Within the 50 states there are 50 experimental labs searching for excellence among our public and private schools. Rhode Island may be attaining a superior math program while Arizona achieves the best science course. Each institution agrees to exchange their successes—one educational plan does not fit all geographical areas. The Federal Department of Education is superfluous in view of the fact that we have a Department of Education in each and every state (not to mention the territories). Freedom of enterprise in business or education creates keen competition and superior results.

Monopolistic government control of education at the federal level, in the near future, may become even more oppressive and/or stagnant. Our Founders understood the dangers of a tyrannical central government. Mind control over the population could eventually subjugate citizens to the undesirable status of servitude created by an unrestrained dictatorial government. Cuba, North Korea and Venezuela, to mention a few, come to mind.

Our very liberty is at issue.

Our brilliant founders understood the dangers of a central government dictating standards; they would have been dismayed by an imposed curricula and self-serving edicts which would compromise the freedom of expression and independent competitive activity by the various states as well as the intellectual control of its citizens.

States in need of funds for educational projects should have long-term loans available with low rates of interest from the U.S. Treasury (if and when necessary). The request for a state educational loan should be made directly to the Treasury Department without bureaucratic interference from Congress.

Educational loan availability, however, would be provided within the federal budget. Furthermore, greater funds would become available to the states for education should "earmarks" or "gifts" be replaced with low interest, long- term loans. Americans don't want politicians to use our hard-earned money to be re-elected.

Politicians would be compelled to rethink grants or earmarks as a positive action if they became loans. The nation must avoid debt thereby conserving our national treasure for useful purposes rather than wasting it on questionable projects and unnecessary interest payments.

Let's allot funds within the Defense Budget to maintain our military academies i.e., West Point, Annapolis, the Air Force, the Coast Guard and the Merchant Marine. A Volunteer National Service Plan, if and when enacted, would draw its funds directly from the Defense Budget, as well. Educational benefits for civil and military services (superior to the G.I. Benefits enjoyed by WWII Veterans) would, once again, maintain the U.S. as the world's most prosperous and secure nation.

Hoarding taxpayer money within the unconstitutional Federal Department of Education, and excessive bureaucracies lacks total common sense. The Federal government should not interfere with the innovations and creativity of the fifty states' Departments of Education. The Federal government should support the achievements of education within the states and not attempt any form of misappropriation or unconstitutional subjugation.

Education is the ultimate key to the nation's prosperity and security.

Lest we forget: The 10th Amendment declares that which is not specified in the Constitution is a right reserved for the state or the people.

An example of rationale funding: Abolishing the Department of Education in 2010 and returning California's share of more than $160 billion would enhance that state's educational funds against any revenue short falls. California, for example, with 12.5% of the nation's population would receive a return of over $20 billion (resolving most of the state's educational necessities). All the states would welcome this particular kind of blessing. Hoarding taxpayer money within the Federal Department of Education is a constitutionally challenged act and lacks total common sense.

The Federal government should not interfere with innovations and the creativity of the fifty state's Departments of Education. The Federal government should support the achievements of education within the states and not attempt any form of unconstitutional subjugation.

Education is the ultimate key to the nation's prosperity and security

Lest we forget: The 10th Amendment declares that which is not specified in the Constitution is a right reserved for the state or the people.

Chapter Thirteen

CONGRESSIONAL BENEFITS REFORM

In a Republic, the people have the power of self determination and lend that power to elected representatives during his or her time in office.

In the private sector it is the employer who determines the final terms and the hiring of an individual for employment. The prospective employee may negotiate conditions and compensation for services rendered but the employer has the last word as to acceptance of the relationship.

In the public sector, employment differs to a degree. The employee is elected to office by his or her constituents. The employers, in this instance, are the American taxpayers also known as constituents. The employers, the constituents, still have the responsibility to set the terms of employment. Relinquishing that responsibility to the office holder is not a good idea for obvious reasons.

It has been the practice, however, for congressional representatives to determine the salaries and compensation for the incoming elected officials— not themselves. Unfair self-service, it was thought, would be avoided by this practice—an unexpected consequence, unfortunately, has occurred. Since 93% of current office holders are being re-elected, practically all of the current incumbents are recipients of the benefit increases they had enacted into law. It would be most appropriate for the employers (the American taxpayers) to determine the salaries and compensations of incumbent office holders. Americans recoil from a stacked deck. A single term limit would have avoided the unexpected consequences, as well.

In any case, A Public Commission made up of constituents and given the title of Commissioners would determine the salaries and benefits for the next group of incoming public officers; including the rules and expenditures for those permitted to travel at government expense i.e., trips to Iraq or Afghanistan, etc. Further, the Commissioners would make the final decisions to acquire private jets and other expenditures requested from members of Congress.

It is a matter of security against corruption to keep the selected Commissioner identities incognito until after their work had been completed. Commissioners could be selected secretly from a group of available people similar to a jury pool. All innovative ideas to keep members of Congress on task and not in pursuit of expensive junkets for pleasure are welcome

The constituents, also known as employers, have the right to remove an office holder for cause via congressional impeachment or they simply could elect another candidate for public office during the next election cycle.

Chapter Fourteen

CONGRESSIONAL CAMPAIGN REFORM

An article during the 2008 presidential election stated that the cumulative cost of the nineteen candidates running for the Presidency of the United States was over $1 billion dollars. The average cost per candidate would have averaged $52.6 million each. A qualified candidate, with fewer funds, may have run out of money before transmitting his or her ideas on an equal-time basis. In 2010, the median income for most American families is between $40,000 and $50,000 a year—a government of, by and for the few with the deepest pockets comes to mind. The very wealthy, the vast resources of a political party and industrial giants would be the only monetarily viable entities to support a candidate for the highest office of the land— the Presidency.

Americans take pride in expressions like fair play, equal rights and opportunity. The traditional American character is founded on the pursuit of egalitarianism or equal opportunity for all. Unless your name is Bill Gates, Donald Trump, Mitt Romney or other Americans who can truthfully say— "Have cash-will run" —the opportunity to compete for public office would require true campaign finance reform and/or the public funding of elections. Access to the airways, such as TV and radio during the campaign season could be made available. All of the above would be equalizers for fair play, equal rights and opportunity.

Folks earning only $50 million a year or less would be hard

pressed to run for the Presidency, as well. Some millionaires would have to mortgage their palatial home or take out a loan, perhaps, to fund a presidential campaign costing $52.6 million or more.

Lobbyists with deep pockets supported many of the candidates. Billionaire, George Soros, philanthropist and lobbyist is as ubiquitous a donor for liberal political causes as could be found on the planet. Mr. Soros has an agenda that, in my view, appears to be moving toward that of a collectivist or a socialist. A great irony has surfaced since he has been an extraordinarily successful capitalist. Is Mr. Soros fearful of rising capatilists displacing his position of power and prestige? Collectivism or Socialism is a two-tier class system: those people who rule and those people who meet the needs of the rulers (A Master-Slave relationship).

Untold numbers of Americans believe excessive campaign contributions or funding is tantamount to a "bribe." How many members of Congress have refused these astronomical campaign contributions, funds or "bribes?" To whom will members of Congress be accountable after receiving humongous campaign contributions, funding or "bribes"? "Those who have the gold—rule".

I am betting on the Constitution. The first Amendment guarantees the freedom of speech—money isn't the last word. Remaining knowledgeable, performing our civic duty and respecting the power of the ballot box are our greatest defenses. Our Founders, also, gave us the Second Amendment should the Republic be threatened.

Don't hold your breath for Congressional support should your $250 dollar contribution become insignificant when competing against $250,000 from a wealthy citizen. Huge industries such as oil, medical, insurance companies, legal firms and international bankers can afford to contribute millions to politicians on both sides of the aisle at the same time during the same election.

Federal programs supporting Social Security, Medicare, prescription drugs and the unconstitutional Federal Department of

Education have been problematic for decades (education is a people and/or state right via the 10th Amendment.) All of the above and foot-dragging on illegal immigration have earned Congress a lower rating than President George W. Bush when he was in office.

There has been very little striving toward solutions. Multiple-term incumbents are more interested, it seems, in Congressional welfare than in what is best for their fellow citizens. Where is the urgency? Hey! Ninety-three percent of these incumbents are re-elected. Why not—they have the "big bucks" behind them—a government of, by, and for the few, once again, comes to mind.

We still have the ballot box. How about electing capable citizens for one four to six year term only? After one term, they, too, will be compelled to live by the laws they have enacted for their fellow man. Governance should be shared by all capable citizens, not monopolized by the few. Our Founders, who were honorable men, understood not all Americans are patriots or parasites. We need a compelling and swift governmental shift like Campaign Reform that pursues a more perfect union…for all the people.

Why have I dwelled on the Federal Reserve and the deep pockets of great industry? Campaign Reform becomes a reality only when we have mitigated the influence of money in electing true patriots. We are presently experiencing abuse by self-interested career politicians who refuse to leave the gravy train. The best way to remove career politicians or parasites is a single Term Limit Amendment of four to six years for all public offices.

Perpetuating American ideals would make the world a safer place. We shall succeed more quickly when we become more proficient in what we profess to be—a viable republic.

Chapter Fifteen

CONGRESSIONAL PROTOCOL REFORM

Why reform an institution that isn't broken? The brilliant and wise Founders devised a check and balance system to counteract the lesser angels of mankind. After two hundred and thirty-three years the system has been thoroughly corrupted. The Congress of the United States is broken. A government of, by and for the people has evolved into a government of, by and for the uncooperative. Congressional approval rating has reached its lowest favorability rating in congressional history—only 11%.

Protocol and tradition have their honored place. Crippling interference with the people's business may initiate new thinking as to the negative effects of current protocol and tradition.

Reserving one side of the congressional chambers for Democrats and the other side for Republicans invites built-in confrontations. Where do the Independents sit? Assuming members of political parties like the Libertarians, the Green Party, the Constitution party or possibly a return of the Reform Party are elected —where would they be seated? It appears to be a form of arrogance and discourtesy. It is unlike the character of Americans to slight fellow Americans who happen to belong to another viable legal party. The Republican Party was once a third Party.

The unresolved problems of Social Security, Medicare and Healthcare have been around for decades, if not longer. A proposal follows that may initiate a start in a positive direction. It will assume loyalty to one's country supercedes party loyalty.

Let's integrate the parties into a common seating arrangement i.e. Democrats, Republicans and Independents sitting side by side. One of two results are possible: The everyday proximity and discourse of a colleague may bring about a more rapid resolve to these long standing problems; or the opposition colleague, due to the side by side seating arrangement, would appreciate convenience and accuracy when within striking distance. The mitigation of violence, however, can be enhanced by the doubling of the Guard or Sergeant at Arms.

Why should the party that prevailed in numbers in the most recent election assume command of all the committee chairmanships? Why not consider the representative, regardless of party, with the greatest ability, experience, expertise, leadership qualities and last, but not least, a reputation for fairness? Any Chair person can be recalled at any time for various reasons, including a member of the opposition party. American citizens would be ecstatic should incumbent Patriots place country first before a political party.

The political whip should be abandoned for at least two reasons: Each Representative must vote his or her conscience and not be troubled with party financial support for re-election. A Term Limit Amendment, in fact, would make the party whip virtually powerless. Office holders would have only four to six years to leave a positive legacy — not 30 or 40 years.

Political funds for re-election would be a non-issue since there would not be a second term. Further, a single term means time would be focused on the issues and not wasted raising funds for the next campaign season.

Once again, a private commission after interviewing congressional members could come-up with new standards that will enhance cooperation and getting the job done with-in a reasonable time frame.

Chapter Sixteen

CONTRACT WITH AMERICA FOR THE 21ST CENTURY

PROBLEM: The greatest American enemy, at this time, is not Iran, North Korea or even al Qaeda. The greatest enemy is entrenched within our borders. It is the alleged corrupt and controversial bank known fallaciously as the "Federal Reserve." The Federal Reserve is a private corporation of international bankers which has controlled our financial destiny since 1913. Mostly foreigners own the Federal Reserve. Google the web for a list of the owners or view Chapter One, "The American Manifesto" (page 18 in this book).

The alleged "Feds" claim we owe them more than 13 trillion dollars; their claim was based on fiat currency given to the United States in the form of loans. We, as tax payers, are paying interest on those loans. The "Feds" have never been scrutinized or audited to determine the true value of the fiat currency (fiat currency is a note or paper that declares by decree or faith only that it is worth what is stated i.e. your dollar bill is not actual money it is referred to as a "Federal Reserve Note" that supposedly represents the value of the denomination on the bill. Think of it as a valid IOU which can be exchanged for value). The true value of fiat currency can go up or down depending on the number of Federal Reserve Notes in circulation creating inflation or deflation. The fiat currency may have been rung up "electronically" as a further bad debt of the United States government.

Without an audit, however, the fiat currency may have a net worth of zero. Monopoly money may have a greater value.

Fact: Precious commodities such as gold and silver support most of the world's currencies. Research bears out there is not sufficient gold or silver in the entire world to support 13 trillion dollars. The conclusion must be "alleged" criminal counterfeiting which is a felonious crime. In fact, the age old practice of fractional banking, in my opinion, is a felonious crime. Why the bankers haven't been charged is a mystery unless law enforcement has been "subsidized" or simply lax in enforcement—you decide.

If an audit cannot backup the true value of the fiat currency used as loans to the United States—we owe the "Feds" nothing. The Federal Reserve is responsible for the Great Depression, the most recent recession and numerous financial distresses too numerous for inclusion. The adjective "alleged" is not necessary when it comes to financial disasters.

SOLUTION: Vote for candidates who will vow to: present, promote, and vote for the following issues—including the expulsion of the nefarious and phony Federal Reserve from our shores—it is not an American bank (see note @ end of article):

1. Repeal the Federal Reserve Act of 1913 and re-institute the U.S. Treasury to resume our banking needs as formerly provided in the constitution under Article 1, Section 8.

2. Enact a single term limit of 4 to 6 years for all elected officials. The president is limited-how about the "good old boys and girls"?

3. Repeal the Income Tax (the 16th Amendment) and re-enact the Ad Valorum tax of 1912 or a Business Tax based on 6% of the GDP. Limit the percentage of the Gross Domestic Product or the GDP to 10% or less.

In 1912, individuals did not pay a direct income tax — it was unconstitutional under that particular tax code. Corporations and companies were the only entities assessed for the Ad Valorum tax.

Instituting a Business Tax for corporations and companies only at 10% of the Gross Domestic Product would have resulted in 1.42 trilliion dollars for the year 2010.

$1.42 trillion dollars is a sum capable of supporting even the most wasteful budget in American history. A recent study by TV/radio commentator Glenn Beck's research team estimated the federal government's waste at more than 50%. That's our money and we can make better use of it. Take-home pay would increase by more than 40%. The U.S. government living within its budgetary limits will limit the waste as well. A ten percent limit of the GDP is more than enough in 2010—congress must learn to live within its means (like the rest of us).

Fact: The percentage of the GDP for government spending in 1912 was less than 3 percent; today, in 2010, the GDP of government spending is more than 30 percent and climbing.

The unconstitutional Department of Education has usurped $162 billion dollars from state governments. All fifty states would have a balanced budget if the Federal Department of Education would return those sums to the states; and, then respect the constitution and disappear.

A single term limit of four to six years would attract patriots to serve for duty and honor—not parasites for self-interest, corruption, power and eventual consummate disgrace.

A shorter and single term compels incumbents to live by the same rules they enact for their fellow Americans—30 plus years of public office is non-sense and contrary to American values—leadership and duty must be shared. We fought a Revolutionary War to resist a permanent group of elitist rulers. The Founders understood power without limits is dangerous. Lobbyists must be registered and controlled.

It is inappropriate for members of congress, our employees, to set the terms of their employment—present or future.

It would be far more consistent in labor relations to create public commissions for:

Congressional Benefits Reform

Congressional Campaign Reform

Congressional Protocol Reform

Individuals reading this book who believe in the issues described in the first paragraph are invited to join the Tea Party movement. Let your local Tea Party organization know that you may be interested, also, in becoming a candidate for public office and desire Tea Party support.

Potential candidates by their pledged honor and signature would be expected to: Present, Promote and Vote for all of the aforementioned issues. Please read and react to the remaining planks of the platform in Chapter 2, page 31 of this book. Your comments are most welcome. Share them with your local Tea Party members. Failure to keep a pledge, naturally, would not go well with fellow Tea Party members.

If interested in joining a Tea party or having Tea Party support as a candidate for public office, once again, send your name, address, E-mail and telephone number to your local Tea Party organization. Contact www.teaparty.org

Go to the Tea Party home page to select your state and city.

Chapter Seventeen

DISTURBING FACTS ABOUT OBAMA AND HIGH OFFICIALS

The President has received enormous campaign contributions from Goldman Sachs ($999,795) and JP Morgan Chase & Co. ($695,132) for a total of $1,889,927. These were funds received beyond campaign limits and allowed because of their status as P.A.C's (Political Action Committees)

Goldman Sachs and JP Morgan Chase & Co. are members of the fallaciously named Federal Reserve. The Federal Reserve is a private corporation of international bankers. Most of their share holders are Europeans. These European bankers have manipulated the American economy since 1913 by virtue of the Federal Reserve Act, the infamous Income tax and its armed, intimidating IRS Agents.

Barack Obama's top contributors are listed on the next page.

Tim Geithner, a former president of the New York Federal Reserve, is currently the Secretary of the Treasury. Geithner is a member of the Trilateral Commission and the Council on Foreign Affairs. One world government is their goal. If successful, the U.S. constitution and American sovereignty would become history. These master money manipulators of the banking industry would reduce the world's working class to consummate serfs. Individual liberties would vanish — American freedom would not appear in future text books.

American members of any "'One World Government" group can not be loyal to the U.S. Constitution and American sovereignty at the same time. Presidents, secretaries of defense and other officials must renounce their affiliation or resign immediately. Globalists such as the Council on Foreign Relations and the Trilateral Commission must be outlawed from service in the United States government.

Loyalty to the U.S. constitution can not be compromised by membership in a group that has as its goal "One World Government" which would destroy our sovereignty. Treason is a capitol offense. Failure to renounce or resign may lead to a firing squad or Impeachment.

Afterthought: President Obama should return all funds received from the Federal Reserve and other "One World" groups. No Problem, he can earn it back after his presidency by becoming a lobbyist for these same groups.

Top Contributors For Barack Obama

The following table lists the top donors to this candidate in the 2008 election cycle. *The organizations themselves did not donate,* rather the money came from the organization's PAC, its individual members or employees or owners, and those individuals' immediate families. Organization totals include subsidiaries and affiliates. Because of contribution limits, organizations that bundle together many individual contributions are often among the top donors to presidential candidates. These contributions can come from the organization's members or employees (and their families). The organization may support one candidate, or hedge its bets by supporting multiple candidates. Groups with national networks of donors – like EMILY's List and Club for Growth - make for particularly big bundlers.

Goldman Sachs

For Goldman Sachs, a large financial investment in President Obama does not appear to be paying off. Wall Street's top investment bank was a generous contributor to Obama's presidential campaign. The company has defended itself from civil fraud charges filed by the Securities and Exchange Commission and, along with the rest of the financial services sector, fended off an aggressive Democratic-led campaign to impose new rules on banks. According to Federal Election Commission figures compiled by the Center for Responsive Politics, Goldman Sachs' political action committee and individual contributors who listed the company as their employer donated $994,795 during 2007 and 2008 to Obama's presidential campaign, the second-highest contribution from a company PAC and company employees. Only the PAC and employees of the University of California, which donated more than $1.5 million, topped Goldman Sachs.

University of California	$1,591,395
Goldman Sachs	$994,795
Harvard University	$854,747
Microsoft Corporation	$833,617
Google Inc	$803,436
Citigroup Inc	$701,290
JPMorgan Chase & Co	$695,132
Time Warner	$590,084
Sidley Austin LLP	$588,598
Stanford University	$586,557
National Amusements Inc	$551,683
UBS AG	$543,219
Wilmerhale Lip	$542,618
Skadden, Arps et al	$530,839
IBM Corp	$528,822
Columbia University	$528,302
Morgan Stanley	$514,881
General Electric	$499,130
US Government	$494,820
Latham & Watkins	$493,835

Federal law prohibits a company from directly giving money to an electoral campaign. Goldman Sachs contributions to the Obama campaign were more than four times larger than the $230,095 in donations to Sen. John McCain's presidential campaign. "Barack Obama's presidential campaign shattered all records when it came to fundraising, so it's no surprise that he significantly outraised John McCain when it came to contributions from the financial industry in general and Goldman Sachs in particular," CNN Deputy Political Director Paul Steinhauser said.

Steinhauser added: "And even though some of the policies he was pushing during his bid for the White House were not so popular with Wall Street executives, it seemed investors wanted to back a winner." According to figures dating to 1990, Goldman Sachs' PAC and employees have consistently contributed more money to Democratic rather than Republican candidates for federal office. In the 2008 election, three out of every four dollars contributed by Goldman Sachs went to Democrats. Since the 2008 election, FEC reports indicate that Goldman Sachs has contributed generously to Senate Banking Committee and House Financial Services Committee members. The two panels are responsible for oversight of the industry.

Morgan Stanley

Morgan Stanley is one of the world's top investment banks, offering its clients everything from stock portfolio management to credit services. Like others in the securities industry, however, it lobbied for money from the federal government in 2008 and 2009 when the industry—along with the economy—was floundering. The investment bank received billions in taxpayer money from the bailout bill. Morgan Stanley invests in and advises virtually every industry affected by federal legislation. The company, which splits its contributions evenly between Democrats and Republicans, has been a major proponent of privatizing Social Security. Morgan Stanley also has lobbied in favor of proposals to deregulate the securities industry, so that investment firms can further extend their reach into financial services.

The enormous funds required to run for public office could be discouraging to less affluent citizens with modest incomes such as firemen, teachers, police officers, electrical contractors, stay-at-home spouses or college professors, like Albert Einstein. The average cost of running for congress these days is one million dollars. Public financing and the availability of time on the media (T.V. and radio) as well as in the local newspapers would be a start in a more inclusive direction for financially stressed candidates. Public sponsored debates for all qualified candidates would permit a greater equalization of participation from all walks of life in America. *Let's create greater opportunities for more Americans to realize the opportunity to serve their nation.*

Chapter 18

SOCIAL SECURITY: A PONZI SCHEME BEYOND COMPARE

It is estimated that Social Security is in debt to the tune of more than 56 trillion dollars of unfunded liabilities. It appears that trillions of dollars have been taken out of the Social Security Trust Fund by members of congress to pay for other national expenditures. These trust funds were replaced by I.O.U. notes. The trust fund is empty except for the current funds taken out of our paychecks every payday. The interest that should have contributed to our trust fund is non-existent. In the private sector such manipulation would have been cause for jail time.

Social Security is an entitlement that was established in 1935 during the Great Depression to protect the indigent Americans created by the Great Depression and politicians seeking re-election. Most Americans, including the wealthy, are now entitled to these funds. It is very telling that members of congress have their own private retirement plans. Entitlements such as Social Security, Medicare, Medicaid and education are contrary to the Founder's constitutional intent. The responsibility of taking care of the aged including medical assistance and education is a people or state right. The federal government is prohibited by the constitution from this responsibility. The Founders understood it would lead to bankruptcy. We should have such wise men in our contemporary congress. Let's remember to vote out the spendthrifts at the very next election.

Members of congress have used a good part of these Social Security funds to be re-elected by a practice called earmarks. Billions of dollars were expended by members of congress to be re-elected by promising and bringing expensive projects to their constituents. How fair is it for an incumbent to have billions of dollars in projects at their disposal for re-election against a competing office seeker?

What can we do for all Americans who have been betrayed by members of congress? We are broke. Possible solutions: Cut government spending to the level necessary to support current Social Security beneficiaries and those about to retire. Reduce governmental staff and pay to reflect the pay in the private sector for similar occupations. The government is over-staffed and overpaid. Let's start with eliminating at least 10% of the work force. In addition, let's reduce 10% to 20% from government salaries. One study shows a government worker receiving 25% more than a counterpart in the private sector. Salary reductions should include members of congress. Eliminate the czars, who were not confirmed by the Senate, and their six figure salaries. Eliminate billions of dollars for earmarks. Eliminate unconstitutional departments such as the Federal Department of Education. Eliminate all duplicative bureaucracies which exist at the state level i.e. the Dept. of Energy. To meet constitutional standards transfer all entitlement programs to the states, along with the funds. State officials may be more easily monitored. The Federal government would be relieved of more than 50% of its obligations in a generation.

Enact a law permitting today's 20 year olds to have the same private retirement programs available to members of congress.

These 20 year olds would not contribute to the constitutionally challenged and failed Social Security program. All retirement programs should be insured. In 25 years or so- after meeting our obligation to the current Social Security recipients-Social Security would become history. The greatest Ponzi scheme of all time would become a dead issue.

PART 2

AUTHOR'S LETTERS TO THE EDITORS

Included in Part II are the author's letters to the editors of various publications. Editors, more often than not, will print or publish an article without notifying an author. Several articles have been published. Other articles, I'm fairly assured, have not. Conservative points of view are not too popular in the main stream press. Articles may have been rejected for good editorial cause, as well. The articles, in any event, were written with unequivocal strong personal conviction.

The letters are arranged according to the dates they were typed. The first article was written in 2006. Some of the paramount issues will have the following titles:

"An Attack on the Second Amendment"

"The Greatest President since Abe Lincoln"

"A Proposed Health Plan: Will Seniors Opt for the Ice Floe?"

"The Federal Reserve"

"Over-Taxation"

"Is the Federal Reserve Necessary?"

THE GREAT AMERICAN BETRAYAL

Critics of President Bush have said that they support our troops, yet degrade the Commander-in-Chief at every opportunity. Failing to understand the need, not only for loyalty to our fighting men and women, but the Commander-in-Chief, as well, is counter-productive. It is unconsionably immoral to knowingly undermine the Commander-in-Chief for political gain. Personal ambition and political power take precedence, it seems, over the loss of American lives as evidenced by their untimely words and deeds.

Undermining the Commander-in-Chief, the President of the United States, alerts an intelligent enemy to division in our government and triggers a delay in our pursuit towards victory. This gives the enemy hope and, consequently, the terrorists continue their efforts prolonging the conflict. The longer the conflict, the greater is the loss of American blood and treasure.

The Commander-in-Chief is our foremost trooper. The officers, men and women who are fighting in Iraq and Afghanistan must see their primary leader as courageous, unwavering and pursuing a noble cause of action. The correctness of the conflict shall be decided by future historians. Politicians maneuvering to gain an advantage for the next election are disgraceful and must butt-out to save the lives of our troopers.

A united and loyal front are what the country requires at this time. There is no doubt that most of the American people understand the mission and do support our troops and their Commander-in-Chief.

For those who opposed the conflict in Iraq for whatever reasons, must not be deterred from the consequences of the 9/11 attack on American soil by al Qaeda. The Afghanistan's Taliban sheltered these terrorists. After 9/11, the Congress and the President of the United States were as one in the condemnation of the perpetrators, al Qaeda and the Afghan Taliban, who supported these killers. Losing upwards to 3,000 innocent humans in a single blow on American soil sends a clear message: Fight or Die. We have no choice but to be in Afghanistan. History will determine the wisdom of attacking Iraq.

Saddam Hussein has been flaunting the world community for years and has used weapons of mass destruction on his own people. There appears to be evidence recently acquired that he transferred much of his weapons to Syria prior to the Iraq conflict and had plans to rearm after the U.N. inspectors had left. Why is that fact not reported in the main media?

After the downfall of Saddam, Iraqis have demonstrated courage and determination to be a free society—millions have gone to the polls for a democratic Iraq.

The mission, many times declared by the President, is to train Iraqis to protect themselves. Our troops, then, may leave with honor and the knowledge that the U.S. sacrifices today may have saved millions of lives in the future.

Let's elect and/or re-elect only those political leaders who understand the significance of unity through loyalty; and, save the lives of our fighting forces by shortening our time and role in the volatile area known as the Middle East. The vast majority of senators are honorable and supportive—for example, Joe Lieberman, a Democrat, and John McCain, a Republican. In the critical next election, do not vote Independent, Democratic, or Republican. Vote as a conscientious, loyal American to support all the troops, which includes the Commander-in-Chief. I personally disagree with some of the President's issues but not issues undermining wartime unity. Bush-bashers beware—he's right about fighting the radicals over there in Afghanistan rather than over here. Unity and loyalty saves lives. Let's all get on board.

—S. Terrusa
5-19-2006

UNITED WE STAND...
DIVIDED WE FALL

Six retired Generals are critical of the war in Iraq and their Commander-in-Chief. A few of them are writing books expressing their point of view, and perhaps gaining a little profit for their efforts.

None of them, to my knowledge, have chosen the path of General Billy Mitchell. While still in active military service and his career at stake, Mitchell was court-martialed for his vigorous confrontation with the top brass of the times. General Douglas MacArthur was his primary antagonist. Billy Mitchell argued assertively the value of constructing aircraft carriers for the fleet prior to World War II. Mitchell was court-martialed for his vigorous defense of aircraft carriers for the navy. Mitchell was exonerated with commendations after his death. Aircraft carriers and fighter bombers destroyed the Japanese fleet in the Pacific, contributing to an earlier than expected victory in WWII. This led to millions of lives being spared on both sides of the conflict.

As an American, I am grateful for the service of these dissenting generals but I question their judgment, motives, values and timing while we are at war. The majority of Generals have supported the Commander-in-Chief and the troops.

There is a saying in the military and in football: "Don't let the enemy know you're hurt." Attacking our Commander-in-Chief during times of war signals to the enemy that we are divided and vulnerable. They would perceive weakness, giving them hope for victory. Prolongation of the conflict becomes inevitable, resulting in a greater loss of lives. Remaining united destroys an enemy, shortens the war and saves American lives.

Why a war in Afghanistan? The death of thousands of our fellow Americans on September 11, 2001 unequivocally demonstrates we must confront a vicious, merciless and determined enemy. Their hatred of our values dominates their will to kill American men, women and children. We can fight them on our soil or in their own backyard. Should they acquire nuclear capability, millions of American lives would be lost—not thousands. Freedom, as we know it, would be forever altered with a nuclear option available to these killers. I truly believe that their top radical leadership is exploiting the Islamic religion and people for their own irrational lust for power and greed. If they truly believe in their religious doctrine that "infidels" must die—we have no choice but to defend ourselves.

After our troops leave Iraq, trained Iraqi troops and police can mop up what remains of these pathological, tyrannical and ruthless religious fanatics. Determination by our Commander-in-Chief, President Bush, the troops and the support of the American people will bring our warriors home sooner rather than later.

Each generation, it seems, must pay the price for securing our liberty. Let's fight them on their own real estate. It's all about, as you well know, location, location, location. God Bless Our Troops and their Commander-in-Chief.

—S. Terrusa
5-19- 2006

HOW TO WIN IN IRAQ AND AFGHANISTAN

Our survival as a nation requires that we become a united force to successfully defend ourselves. The dissenion to date mitigates the morale of our fighting forces. An unpopular war is in progress—we can support the troops or abandon their efforts—the choice is clear. We cannot support the troops and ask them to lay down their arms at the same moment.

To be united we must resolve our nation's priorities. Our representatives, right or wrong, agreed to pursue the wars in Afghanistan and Iraq. Many of us, for whatever reasons, are for the Iraq war, against the war, disappointed in the progress or lack of progress of the Iraq war, depending on what one chooses to believe about the war. Let's not be distracted, however, by those who attempt to divide us. A united effort is urgent.

We can all agree that our military has performed with skill, courage and honor. We take pride in their accomplishments and they continue to earn our respect. Our troops do, indeed, deserve our support. The United States is most successful when we are all part of a united force.

A football team divided in respect for its coach has little or no chance in defeating an opponent. The military, fortunately, is not as divided as their fellow citizens. Let's all truly support the troops and the war effort by supporting their Commander-in-Chief as well. Public dissent, in time of war, places our troops in harm's way. Never let the enemy know our internal conflicts, thereby giving them hope for success and/or prolonging the war effort. A sustained war causes an unnecessary loss of life.

Over 2,600 fellow Americans have died to date believing that they were securing the liberties which we continue to enjoy and that some of us take for granted. The irony is that freedom is not free. Millions of Americans fought and died in the past to preserve these precious liberties that we claim as the rights of all Americans.

Supporting our troops loses its meaning when we fail to honor their sacrifices by leaving the conflict before Iraqis and Afghans can defend themselves.

Americans take pride in keeping our promises and never retreat when the cause is just. This may result in the freedom of some old enemies becoming our newest friends. Japan and Germany are historical facts; they were old enemies and now our friends. These are facts that bode well for Iraq and Afghanistan as well as the United States.

Giving the Iraqis and Afghans the opportunity to become stable democratic governments in the Middle East mitigates the dangers of our enemies becoming a greater threat. Possession of nuclear weapons for a safer world must be controlled worldwide. An uncontrolled and avowed enemy with nuclear capabilities could result in the loss of millions of American lives—not thousands. After our troops come home, the Iraqis and Afghans will be responsible for their own security and destinies.

Talk with your fellow Americans with the intent of unity, the realistic support of our troops while they are still fighting, and the quickest way to get them home with honor. Let's support our newest allies, bearing in mind that Iraq and Afghanistan troops become our first line of defense against terroristic tyrants exploiting the Islamic religion and intimidating Islamic moderates.

Radical Islamics disrespect every religion but their own. This kind of arrogance and misguided obsession is deadly. The radicals also believe that if you are an infidel who refuses to convert to Islam, then you must die. The radical interpretation of Islam creates fear among the moderate Islamic. The moderate Islamic, out of fear, thus far has shown very little resistance to these bullies and murderous tyrants. In the Declaration of Independence, "Life, liberty and the pursuit of happiness…" does not permit a religion that would kill "infidels" as members of our population. Moderate Muslims must deny the killing of so-called infidels to become true Americans. Religious freedom in the United States does not mean you can "kill" your fellow American.

In the name of our children and grandchildren's future, let's agree today on a common course of action. Decide which candidates can achieve victory for us when you cast your ballot in November.

—Sal Terrusa
6-20-2006

A THANKSGIVING DAY FOR ENDURING FREEDOM

Thanksgiving should be a daily ritual. Our blessings are too numerous to give each and every one of them the degree of gratitude they deserve on a single day of the year. The greatest blessing of all, in my view, is to be an American enjoying freedoms most people on the planet can only imagine.

We owe our fellow Americans, past and present, a respect and duty for their success in keeping us a free nation. The respect for their willingness to sacrifice their blood becomes our duty to maintain the freedoms they had so gallantly won. In answering the nation's call to engage in battle—fallen Americans and American survivors have made this day of thanksgiving possible.

The greatest threat to our liberties may come from within as well as from a foreign foe. Each generation has a responsibility to identify and resist the gravest threat to our American system of values; which enemy or enemies must we confront who pose an optimum threat to the nation's security and prosperity? The Security of a nation relies on its prosperity to maintain its armed forces. Simply put –no prosperity –no military capable of defense.

We have an enemy within, threatening our economic survival, which must be confronted—if we are to survive as a Republic. The alternative is the tyranny of collectivists, namely, fascism, socialism, communism and international bankers or an attempt to install martial law and the usual ensuing dictatorship. Americans are an astute people and none of the above is likely to happen, especially, if we resolve the problem in a timely manner.

A warning: Unlimited taxation, of any kind, leads to unlimited power and the loss of our liberties. Resist all attempts to censor or tax the internet. Knowledge is power.

A packet of information has been prepared to inform your generation of an imminent threat and what can be done about it. Several other issues have been included contributing to President Lincoln's hope for "...a more perfect union."

All Americans have a right to view problematic issues and determine their solutions as they see fit. It is my fervent wish, after reading the information in the packet, that your generation will act effectively and with great alacrity. I am extremely proud of my family.

You all have my love and best wishes for your success,

—Sal Terrusa

Enclosed: National Priorities

For all patriots not present at our family celebration: National Priorities is accessible via watchdogsforcommonsense.net A recommended course of action: E-mail any and all credible political messages to your friends and relatives and have them foreword the same... and so on.

This thanksgiving message was given to members of the Terrusa family and friends on 11-24-2008.

FAIR PLAY: AN AMERICAN TRADITION

A recent article stated that the cumulative cost of the nineteen candidates running for the Presidency of the United States in 2008 was over $1 billion dollars. This would place the average cost per candidate at $52.6 million each. Folks earning only $50 million a year or less would be hard pressed to run for the presidency as well. Some millionaires would have to mortgage their home or homes and/or take out a loan, perhaps, to fund a presidential campaign costing $52.6 million or more.

Lobbyists with deep pockets such as billionaire, George Soros, are supporting many of the candidates. Mr. Soros is as ubiquitous as Cindy Sheehan and has an agenda, in my view, which is moving toward collectivism or Socialism. Ironically, he has been an extraordinarily successful capitalist. Socialism is a two-tier system: those who rule and those who serve the needs of the rulers. Serfs, who till their own land, would have a better chance for economic survival than an unemployed modern worker.

Excessive campaign funding is tantamount to a "bribe." What member of Congress has refused these astronomical campaign funds? Who, in government, is beholding to the sincere interest of less affluent Americans? Why have significant issues dragged on for decades? It appears a qualified candidate with fewer funds may run out of money before transmitting his or her ideas on an equal-time basis. The median income for most American families is between $40,000 and $50,000 a year—a government of, by and for the few comes to mind. A determined candidate, with fewer assets, could mortgage the house, encourage a spouse to take a second job and put the kids up for adoption. It only takes about a million dollars to run for a congressional seat. It appears only doctors, attorneys, wealthy Americans and community organizers can afford to run for public office. Mr. Soros contributed heavily to President Obama's campaign.

Americans take pride in expressions like fair play, equal opportunity and inalienable rights. Far too often, Americans have experienced "inalienable frights." The traditional American character is founded in the pursuit of egalitarianism. Unless your name is Bill Gates, Warren Buffet or Donald Trump the opportunity to compete for public office would require true campaign finance reform and/or the public funding of elections. Access to the airways, that is TV and radio, during the campaign season may also be an equalizer.

Excessive campaign funding is tantamount to a "bribe." What member of Congress has refused these astronomical campaign funds? Who, in government, is beholding to the interest of less affluent Americans? Why have significant issues dragged on for decades? Federal programs supporting Social Security, Medicare, prescription drugs and the unconstitutional[i] Department of Education have been problematic for generations. All of the above and, now, foot-dragging on illegal immigration, have earned Congress a lower rating than President Obama.

There is very little striving toward solutions—multiple-term incumbents are more interested, it seems, in Congressional welfare than in what is best for their fellow citizens. Where is the urgency? Hey! Ninety-three percent of these incumbents are re-elected. Why not—they have the "big bucks" behind them. A government by the few and for the few has compromised our check and balance system.

We still have the ballot box… How about electing capable citizens for one term only? A Term Limit Amendment could be for one term only. After one term, they, too, would live by the laws they have enacted. The one term could be between 4 to 6 years for all elected officials. Governance should be shared by all capable citizens, not monopolized by the few. Our forefathers, who were honorable men, understood not all Americans are patriots or parasites; these extremely wise men included a term limit in the constitution. The term limit was ignored as Congress voted increased benefits for the next Congress, which happened to be 93% of the current Congress. We need a compelling and swift governmental shift that pursues a more perfect union...for all the people.

Equal opportunity to succeed in business or politics for all Americans is fair play and an American Tradition.

Promoting American ideals around the world shall succeed more quickly when our nation becomes more proficient in what we profess to be—a viable republic.

—S. Terrusa

[i] Education is a people and/or state right via the 10th Amendment

AN ATTACK ON THE SECOND AMENDMENT

Attorney General Eric Holder is challenging the Second Amendment by advocating no citizen should have the right to own an "assault weapon". The initial reaction by most Americans — No Big Deal! Who needs an assault weapon, anyway? It is a Big Deal! By setting a legal precedent defining what kind of weapon an American can or cannot own would eventually destroy the right to bear arms. The right to bear arms is not only a constitutional right, more importantly, it is a natural right to defend one's self against people or governments that would do us harm (domestic as well as foreign).

In legal terms, the logic pursued might proceed as follows — since we (the government) have successfully banned assault weapons, the precedent has been set to ban any weapon a government of the present or the future may decide is against the public or the government's interest. Attacking any part of the Second Amendment would eventually and effectively strip Americans of their right to bear arms.

Gaining our freedom and independence from the British Empire required an act of war. Most Americans owned guns for hunting and self-protection. American soldiers often carried their own weapons to battle British regulars. The guns of American citizens supported the effort to defeat the British (the world's greatest army at the time).

What protection would the American people have should a government ban hunting rifles, target pistols, shotguns or any weapon designed for self-protection? Americans are in possession of many dangerous devices that are equally lethal depending on their use: Kitchen knives, hammers, ice picks, axes, bows and arrows and, lest we forget, golf clubs (especially on a frustrating round of golf). Why not ban these potentially lethal objects? How many more murders have been committed with a butcher knife, a switch blade or blunt instruments like a crowbar or baseball bat? Why not outlaw all of the aforementioned devices? David slew Goliath with a sling; what chance would David have had without it? Why not outlaw the sling shot? Ridiculous! Most Americans would agree such courses of action would be impractical and, frankly, contrary to common sense.

The most lethal instrument of death and destruction killed over 43,000 people in 2007. The automobiles' destruction of human life and property dwarfs the losses committed by the gun. The automobile, an apparent necessity for the American lifestyle, relies on driver training safety, personal responsibility and laws to punish the offenders. The way people use their weapons, utensils and automobiles should be our focus –- not a nonsensical ban regardless of their lawful utility or constitutional right. The safe and expert use of a weapon through training and certification by private or public organizations must be available, i.e. the NRA, the military, shooting ranges, etc.

Some Americans own warplanes, tanks and heavy weapons of war as collectors or as owners of a private museum. How many more freedoms would Mr. Holder consider usurping in making the people of the United States powerless to defend themselves against the tyranny of a future despotic government or a foreign invader? The dominance of "Big Brother" would end the creativity of individual expression or what we used to call freedom. Our constitutional freedoms have been won by the spilling of American blood. Let's spare the next generation.

We must not allow any entity to take away our right to self-defense by banning weapons. We must punish those, however, for the misuse of a weapon or a device used as a weapon. Criminals will always manage to obtain a gun (i.e., the black market, theft, etc.). Law-abiding citizens would be unable to defend themselves or their loved ones without the right to own a weapon. Without a weapon for self-defense your entire family might perish. Why allow the criminal the exclusive choice to decide who will live and who will die? It takes ten and one half minutes for the police to respond to a 911 call in the city of Los Angeles. Angelinos and family members would be at the mercy of the criminal during that period. In London, crime went up 40% after a ban on handguns was enacted.

The right to bear arms includes the ability to defend one's self against all enemies, foreign or domestic. Foreign invaders would be met by millions of Americans who have guns and know how to use them. A U.S. government that attempted tyranny over its free citizens would also be met by these same guns; at this point, we may need an assault weapon, a machine gun, a grenade-launcher or a confiscated tank or two.

Americans need their guns for lawful pursuits and the defense of freedom. We have the natural and constitutional right to use these guns against criminality and enslavement. The Second Amendment guarantees all of our natural rights. The Second Amendment provides an equal opportunity for criminals and tyrants to experience "victimhood" (when citizens exercise their right to self defense).

"When the people fear their government, we have tyranny. When the government fears the people, we have freedom."

— *Thomas Jefferson*

PATRIOT PAPERS / Part 2

The Attorney General, Eric Holder, wants to ban the assault weapon (an attack on the second amendment). President Obama must have a chat with Mr. Holder; reminding the Attorney General– resignation, dismissal or impeachment is in order for any appointed or elected official ignoring his or her pledge to support the Second Amendment of the constitution.

—Sal Terrusa
3-11-2009

THE FEDERAL RESERVE

The questionable but alleged "legal practices" of international bankers has led to economic disaster several times in our history. The Great Depression is a prime example. We are, once again, in the clutches of the monopolistic money mongers by enduring the current financial crisis of 2008-2010. The Federal Reserve is a private international cartel of bankers which has controlled our financial destiny since 1913. The phrase, "Federal Reserve," was intended to mislead the American people into believing it was an American bank— it is not.

It is the conviction of many enlightened Americans that these money manipulators are the greatest enemies to our financial destiny. The alleged "Federal Reserve" owes its primary allegiance to its foreign shareholders — not the American taxpayer. The Federal Reserve and its mostly foreign shareholders receive the profits. The shareholders and the Federal Reserve are the beneficiaries and, as taxpayers, we become the victims.

The first order of business is to return the formerly constitutional creation of currency and the setting of interest rates to the U.S. Treasury (article 1, Section 8).

The conspiratorial means of deception, fraud and counterfeiting of money to which these foreign bankers refer to as a Federal Reserve Note must be legally challenged. The Federal Reserve Note is fiat money. Court decisions, in abundance, have declared the Federal Reserve Note is not money. By abolishing the Federal Reserve and restoring the U.S. Treasury — we could pay off our debt to the Federal Reserve with American fiat money. The U.S. has assets of oil, coal and natural gas (under our territory)and productive activity that more than equals the national debt.

Mr. Bernanke, the most powerful financial leader in the world, has been re-elected to the chairmanship of the Federal Reserve (once again, an international cartel of private bankers). When confidence in the money supply weakens or is destroyed—Mr. Bernanke and his cohorts—will have the legal right to take your property and just about everything else you may have owned at one time. Shades of 1929! No earthly man or woman should have that kind of financial power.

We are rapidly moving towards 14 trillion dollars of debt and facing economic collapse, similar to Greece, unless we stop the wasteful spending and create jobs by significantly lowering taxes. The only winners in a contrived economy are the international banking cartels of which the alleged Federal Reserve is a primary beneficiary, financial predator or both.

The Federal Reserve contributed to President Wilson's campaign of 1912. President Wilson demonstrated his gratitude by signing the Federal Reserve Act of 1913.

The President realized his folly, too late, and publicly lamented—"I have ruined my country." No greater truth had been spoken.

I refer you to the "History of the Federal Reserve" by G. Edward Griffin and Dr. Ken Motto's, "The Federal Reserve: History of Lies, Thievery, and Deceit."

What other Presidents have been influenced by untold contributions from these arcane and wealthiest of international lobbyists? How many Presidents, besides Wilson, have dishonored their office? Presidents of the United States must be beyond reproach. It may be time for a congressional investigation; a public commission of highly trusted Americans may be a superior idea. Why not clear the air and, in the spirit of cleaning house, let's find out which one of our presidents has been naughty or nice. Some folks may consider "Naughty" as a euphemism for treason. There are always, at least, two sides to a story.

More than a few presidents have been assassinated, while in office, who opposed these international central banks. The alleged victims were James Garfield, William McKinley and John F. Kennedy. Some may hold that the assassinations were coincidental. We may never know. Andrew Jackson, we do know, survived two attacks after he fired over 700 hundred federal employees associated with the central bank. Abe Lincoln was assassinated, as well. President Lincoln refused to deal with these foreign banks because they wanted to charge between 24% and 36% for much needed loans to finance the civil war. He created currency known as "greenbacks" to pay down the war debt. John Wilkes Booth was his assassin. Was this assassination also coincidental? What say you?

Thomas Jefferson wisely refused to renew the charter for the central bank at the end of his presidency. The charter was renewed, however, as soon as the next president moved into the white House. Most Americans, unlike the profligate central banks, cannot compete monetarily to support politicians for their re-elections. The well-healed lobbyists and the phony "Federal Reserve" (alluding to their fallacious title) with their ability to print money and set interest rates, without restraint, have a decided advantage.

These private international bankers are involved with nations all over the world. How can we trust a conglomerate of self-serving private bankers, maximizing their profits, and whose primary fiduciary loyalty must be to their foreign shareholders and not the American taxpayer?

THE MAFIA TAKES OVER TERRITORIES—INTERNATIONAL OR CENTRAL BANKS TAKE OVER COUNTRIES.

Any member of the Congress, the Senate, or the White House

failing to repeal the Federal Reserve Act of 1913 should be ousted from public office. Many of our politicians accept contributions from the so-called "Feds" for their re-election. Failure to remove these political parasites from office may lead to the economic serfdom of the 1930's or worse. These self-serving "Gutless" career politicians must disappear at the very next election. It's very easy—all it takes is your enlightened vote—monitor their voting actions in congress and the names of their contributors. It never hurts to limit them to a single term—which should be the new norm.

A warning—major contributors, to avoid identification, will funnel funds through third parties. Congressional popularity is at its lowest point in decades (14%)—it may be time to turn out all incumbents, regardless of party, to let our mis-representatives know who is really in charge of the Republic.

WE ALREADY KNOW THE FEDERAL RESERVE MUST GO.

—Sal Terrusa
3-21-2010

THE GREATEST PRESIDENT... SINCE ABE LINCOLN

The greatest President—since Abe Lincoln—would sustain the United States as the world's most powerful military and restore its status as the most prosperous. National security would be assured by a prospering nation able to support such a military. A great president understands the needs of his country must come first. There is no title, such as President of the World, in our constitution.

Prosperity, under a capitalistic system, would be enhanced by a plethora of viable consumers—it is these consumers who would spend and expand the economy. Businesses, large and small, are the genuine creators of wealth—not the federal government. Big government spending on wasteful programs is outrageous. For example: Social Security and Medicare have been dismal economic failures—trillions of dollars of unfunded liabilities will impact future generations. Continued irrational governmental economic mismanagement will doom American prosperity and diminish national security—a bankrupt United States must be avoided. Solutions—stop the spending and enact a new tax code which allows more take-home pay.

Doc Holiday would not gamble on the new national healthcare bill after seeing the kind of hands Uncle Sam's congressional relatives have been dealing lately.

Congressional common sense is A.W.O.L. and or corrupt—

the choice is yours.

Spending taxpayers' money for projects in congressional districts intended to optimize re-election for an officeholder is immoral, un-American and "legal theft". Earmarks are out-of-control. The Constitution enumerates 21 rights of the federal government in Article I, Section 8—spending taxpayers' money to gain an advantage for re-election is not one of them. Earmarks or "gifts" must be replaced with loans—there should not be the use of "free" taxpayers' money to enhance the re-election of an office holder from any congressional district.

Over-taxation is the primary factor in the diminishment of consumer spending and job loss. Raising taxes is the death knell for a thriving economy—the bailouts for failing businesses i.e., auto manufacturers, insurance companies and banks was an extremely bad idea. The market would have adjusted without wasting or jeopordizing the taxpayers' hard-earned dollars. The current income tax as the engine creating funding for the national government is extremely flawed. Fair trade may be a better idea than Free Trade when critical industries protecting our freedoms, during war-time, are moving off shore.

The Income Tax Amendment of 1913 is anachronistic and deserving of repeal. The Tax Code has over 66,000 pages and continues to grow annually. The income tax is confusing, unfair, inadequate and punitive. The 16th Amendment (the income tax) must be terminated by repeal and replaced with a more sensible tax. A consumer tax on goods permits greater revenues for the federal government and increased spending power for the consumer—a win-win situation.

Only corporations and companies paid taxes as was the practice prior to 1913. The individual did not pay an income tax. Capitation taxes were unconstitutional prior to the advent of the Income Tax. The pre-1913 tax plan, an Ad Valorum Tax, must be restored. It optimized opportunities for all Americans. Over-taxation restricts economic mobility.

Federal entitlements should be transferred to the states along with the revenues. The federal government has proved to be a disastrous money-manager. President Madison ruled against giving funds, not enumerated in the constitution, to a parochial area. Earmarks would have been declared unconstitutional in his time; in fact, it should be ruled unconstitutional in our time. The General Welfare responsibility was intended by the Founders to be the responsibility of the people or the states, not the federal government. How does congress get away with ignoring the constitution? The federal budget would be cut in half by shifting the General Welfare back to the people or the states. A spending limit based on the GDP and approved by the voters would also lower the federal budget.

A tax based on a percentage of the Gross Domestic Product (GDP) rather than income would be fairer, simpler, adequate and non-threatening. Punitive measures such as late penalties, interest, and the confiscation of property and garnishment of wages, along with April 15th would fade into history for the individual. In a pre-1913 tax system—the tax collectors, corporations and businesses, are the only folks subject to fraud or alleged fraud—not the individual.

Examples of the consumer tax based on a percentage of the GDP follows:

In 2006, the GDP was $15.8 trillion. A consumer tax of 5% would have yielded $750 billion dollars annually for the federal budget. A 6% tax on the GDP would have produced $948 billion dollars (more than adequate revenue for past annual budgets). AN UPDATE: On October 19th—the 2009 annual budget was officially 1.41 trillion dollars. Some economists have predicted we will have a 22 trillion dollar GDP in the near future. The good news for consumers—net take-home pay, due to the Pre-1913 tax system would increase by 30 to 40 percent. The decrease in personal taxation would permit individuals to purchase their own private health and pension plans—similar to what members of Congress have provided for themselves (at taxpayers' expense). Americans with sufficient take-home pay to purchase their own medical and retirement plans would avoid further governmental mismanagement and waste.

The government, too, with greater income would be more able to provide subsidies for incapacitated citizens and retraining citizens for higher-paying jobs to meet basic needs. Educational loans would be made available to serious and reliable citizens in need of retraining. Americans should not give away taxpayer contributions for healthy, able-bodied citizens. Public service such as the military and the Peace Corps should qualify students for educational benefits.

As Medicare and Social Security shift to privatization, e.g., health and retirement plans, a more than 45% decrease in the federal budget would occur. Federal taxation would be reduced by mega-billions of dollars. Citizens would resume the responsibility of paying their own debts without "big brother" legally confiscating the fruits of their hard-earned labors. The result would be an even greater increase in prosperity for all Americans, including the government. A growing economy — more revenue for the government.

The greater share of the General Welfare responsibility, if not all, should defer to the states or the people as the Founders intended. Any other course, they understood, would lead to national bankruptcy. It's not enough to read the U.S. Constitution, it must be respected and pursued, as well. The revenues, too, would shift to the states or the people. The states are better equipped to take care of the unique needs of its citizens. The federal government would still be responsible for the defense of the country, interstate and international affairs. States could apply for low-interest, long-term loans from the U.S. Treasury, if necessary. No giveaways, please. A financial reserve for a nation is as sensible as a financial reserve for a family.

BEWARE OF BANKING GLOBALIST—FINANCIAL MANIPULATORS WHO WOULD FORCE FREE CITIZENS INTO SERVITUDE OR SLAVERY—AN UNWANTED MASTER AND SLAVE RELATIONSHIP.

The goal of financial manipulators or globalists is to use organizations, like international banks and the United Nations, to dominate the citizens of the world via control of the vast sums of money generated by the blood and sweat of the world's wage-earners. The U.N. may seek a 1% tax—initially. Watch out! That is the beginning of the end for economic freedom. They will seek more and more as time moves on.

Americans must never surrender its sovereignty to international bankers, foreign organizations, dictators or richer than Allah, oil monopolies such as OPEC.

The best way to defeat the oil barons, who are using their profits to kill our troops, is to drill for domestic oil and reduce or eliminate our enemies' market share.

We can cut back on this kind of competition as soon as we truly develop alternative fuels and infrastructures. Saving the lives of our sons, daughters, husbands, wives, mothers and dads on the battlefield comes—first.

The spill in the gulf will not stop off-shore drilling by any nation so engaged. Oil independence protects our troops and our security. Short-sighted environmentalists who fail to protect their beloved freedom fighters, to the fullest, should be ashamed and ignored —so drill, baby, drill! After a billion years of climate change we should be able to wait a few more years while protecting our heroic defenders. There will be time enough to save the planet. Environmentalist should think about preserving our fellow humans before a nuclear catastrophe places mankind beyond salvation, allowing the human race to become just another extinct species.

It will take time to develop alternative fuels and infrastructure. Some folks believe climate change "fears", by design, will expedite greater control by the United Nations. Trust your commonsense. Still feeling vulnerable!? Let your heart not be troubled and, if still doubtful, there is no substitute for hard work and keeping a close eye on the government.

The Federal Reserve is a private international corporation of bankers—it is not an American governmental bank. The shareholders are mostly foreigners.

A conflict of interest arises—have these international bankers been faithful to the American taxpayers or to their foreign shareholders? I'm betting on the "foreign" shareholders. A U.S. President's constitutional duty is to accommodate the American taxpayer first and foreign shareholders last, if at all. Lest we forget— the Federal Reserve, an international corporation of bankers, is a threat to American sovereignty. The so-called "Feds" would enjoy even greater wealth in a One-World style government.

"Give me liberty or give me dead financial tyrants." Forgive me, Patrick.

A future president, by persuasion, in addition to providing a new tax system based on a limit of the GDP (Gross Domestic Product) to replace the income tax, must repeal the 16th Amendment. Presidential leadership would promote a Balanced Budget Amendment and a Debt Reduction plan. A term-limit amendment would mitigate corruption, as well. Single-term office holders would most likely be patriots—not parasites; especially, if they were compelled to live by the same laws they made for their fellow Americans. A ruling class is definitely—un-American.

The greatest President—since Abe Lincoln—must possess the vision and courage to repudiate and terminate the private international corporation known deceptively as the "Federal Reserve."

The U.S. Treasury, under strict supervision, must retake and control the financial destiny for all Americans as the constitution wisely provided.

A reminder... *"Where the people fear the government you have tyranny; where the government fears the people you have liberty."*
—*Thomas Jefferson*

The greatest President—since Abe Lincoln—has yet to arrive.
—Sal Terrusa
10-28-09
Revised:5-10-10

THE WISDOM OF OUR FATHERS

The late and great comedian, George Carlin, might have said the following, "Want to take the country back? Then let's cut the crap!"

Our brilliant forefathers, while writing the Constitution, created a system of checks and balances, a master stroke, to ensure the Republic's integrity toward a new political experiment.

The power to rule a country would begin with citizens, not the head of state. In a Republic—citizens lend their power to representatives. Citizens are able to withdraw an unsatisfactory choice during the next election cycle or sooner, if necessary. A relatively small group of intelligent, knowledgeable, bold and honorable men understood the nature of man (i. e., the temptation of power to aggrandize one's self-interest at the risk of forsaking the "Common Welfare"). Far too many "career politicians", unfortunately, have corrupted the system.

A major issue, the current energy crisis, is an example of imperfect man making matters worse for their fellow man. The energy crisis, in part, is the result of actions by the petroleum cartel (aka, the OPEC pirates), well-meaning but soft-headed environmentalists, uninformed Americans, and speculators, compounding the catastrophic reality of the energy crunch.

The environmentalists have had noble thoughts in preserving the planet—serenity and beauty for ourselves and our posterity.

It would be difficult to enjoy and or appreciate the preservation of our planet, however, while some of the world's radicals decide it is time to eliminate all infidels, including environmentalist, via a nuclear confrontation.

The loss of thousands of lives in one of our greatest cities, New York, on 9/11 should have been a clue as to their intentions. Our most dangerous enemies on the terrorist list, thus far, are Iran, North Korea and Syria. It may be fair to say Radical Islamic countries would prefer to convert Americans to Islam rather than kill us. Should we refuse to convert to radical Islam and be defeated militarily— very few of us would be left to enhance our posterity. Fight or die seems to be our destiny. The radicals are ready to fight or die.

Presidents Nixon and Carter both foresaw the need for energy independence and warned Congress including the American people over three decades ago. Anyone under 35 years of age, regrettably, did not witness the Pan-Arab oil embargo of 1973; literally hundreds of vehicles waited in line for a limited supply of gasoline (the embargo was intended to punish the United States for supporting the Israelis in the Israel and Arab War—it worked.)

The international monopolistic purveyor of most of the world's oil, OPEC, is crushing the economies, not only of the United States, but virtually every country dependent on this form of energy. After 36 years (since our first warnings), we are not only a nation still at risk but must face the challenges of a declining economy—a failing economy weakens our military as well as our standard of living.

The United States is facing the compelling demands of the newly arrived 21st century— we must have more oil until alternative fuels comes on line. We are in a race for survival. Drilling for oil is the key to undermine our potential oppressors until alternative energies can be developed. The 700 billion dollars we paid to Middle Eastern countries for oil in 2007 could have been spent in oil rich America. Our economy and national security would have been advanced.

Success in the development of alternative energies must be imminent to avoid a deeper crisis. In the interim, we will still require oil for our planes, trains and the huge work horses of industry (the eighteen wheelers). These vehicles are too large to be powered by electric batteries. Further, it will take a decade or two before all of the old clunkers are off the road.

Our dependence on foreign oil placed our nation at risk in 1973 and that risk is still with us in 2009. Purchasing oil from foreigners, who are not our friends, provides them with the profit to kill or maim our troops. Until alternative fuels are available, we must drill in America to save our fighting men and women who stand between us and a deadly foe. A nuclear catastrophe would severely challenge environmentalist to save the planet and the alleged negative impact of the carbon footprint.

The earth's destruction by carbon emissions may take decades or longer, whereas destruction of the earth by nuclear confrontations may be instantaneous and without warning.

Our children and grandchildren deserve a future free from the radical rodents of tyranny and oppression. When Americans eventually awaken, may we and the people of Iran and North Korea survive the doomed destinies of their extremist leaders.

A federal government directed by patriots is the key to getting the job done. Self-serving politicians, who remain in office for 30 or 40 years, must be removed from office at the very next election. Incumbents who are on record to support these issues and others for the past 30 years (but unable to persuade colleagues to their points of view) must not be reelected—they have failed the American people. People who don't earn their pay but enjoy the benefits of public office are known as parasites. A Term Limit Amendment would resolve that problem.

The American people, President Jefferson advised, must review the effectiveness of the government every generation (20-

25 years) and make the necessary changes. The power of the people is the ballot box or, if necessary, the bullet (in the event, domestic tyranny attempts to overthrow the Republic). We have a duty to honor Americans who have fought and died for our principles.

Let your voices be heard at the ballot box. Take your country back!

—Sal Terrusa
8-15-2009

AMERICA: A WORLD CLASS PARADIGM IN CRISIS

Every citizen of the world would be fortunate to live in a nation that pursues unrestrained freedom in a meritorious way, provides an optimal common defense and a sincere effort towards the general welfare.

The United States appears to represent that kind of nation. The United States or America, as it is often referred, attracts millions of immigrants and/or aliens from around the globe (both legal and illegal). The American paradigm supports a relatively modern historical concept that the people have the power of self-governance to determine the relative issues. In a republican form of government citizens lend that power to its elected representatives. This is a revolutionary idea that witnessed its incipiency during the creation of the U.S. federal constitution.

Citizens, with absolute power to choose and direct its leaders, have captured the imaginations of suppressed peoples worldwide. Tyrannical governments are still not extinct. Democracies, fortunately, are rapidly ascending.

The divine right of a king had been challenged during the Magna Carta and, once again, during our Revolutionary war. The unchartered course of a democratic republic had begun. The new nation successfully defeated the British and the tyrant, King George III. The victory paved the way for the new United States

Constitution and the birth of the Republic.

Our Founders advised future generations, however, to periodically review and transform the government by eradicating outmoded practices and adopting the new. The ruling order for the early American Republic was designed to include citizen-legislators, representatives and senators, on a share-the-power basis. The periodic rotation of citizen leaders intended to counter the formation of an excessively powerful and permanent ruling class. The European model of entrenched elitists was to be avoided.

Term limits were set for both chambers; two years for the House of Representatives and six years for the Senate. In the beginning, although it was considered an honor to serve one's country, the pay was low and hardships prevailed. Personal income suffered while away from the farm, business or a profession.

The American paradigm is in crises. Will we meet the challenge? We now have a well- paid ruling class that has ignored the original term limits. We have learned, once again, that unlimited terms lead to absolute power. Absolute power leads to absolute corruption (a para phrase inspired by John Acton). A practical single term limit must be re-imposed—no more than six years for any elected office. The excessive influence of money allows incumbents to remain in office for decades; a factor which has compromised the checks and balances of current day governments. More on a term limit will follow in a separate article entitled, Patriots vs. Parasites: A Case for a Term Limit.

How do we regain control of a government that reflects the will of all the people and counter-balances the excessive power of money which leads to greed and tyranny by and for the few? A review of the issues and proposals to restore our Republic in the tradition of fairness is foremost and forthcoming in future articles. The guiding wisdom of the Gettysburg Address articulated that we are "a government of, by and for the people." The United States was never intended to be a nation... of, by and for the few.

How did the United States become the envy of the world? Economic competition was the stimulus for creativity and unfettered opportunity. Capitalism was the vehicle for incredible advances in American industry. The United States possesses the greatest economy the world has ever witnessed. Financial reverses, however, must be studied and corrected.

In times of recession or depression, the United States is still the leader for greater economic stability. China, India and many third world countries are rapidly emerging towards economic success by embracing capitalism; China has created a hybrid of capitalism and communism (this is not an imprimatur, just a statement of fact). Economic competition lowers prices, improves quality and a higher standard of living. An economic system falters when imprudent policies are allowed to go foreword without oversight and or inferior regulatory practices. The government performs as the prime monitor. When the government fails in its duty – economic chaos is the result. Should a referee, during a sporting event, miss calling a significant penalty – the game could be lost. Our federal officials have failed us in the most recent economic crises which began before the turn of the 21st century.

Pure collectivism, such as socialism or communism, mutes competition and the mobility to move to a higher economic level. The incentives and opportunity for advancement are diminished. The collectivist envies the capitalist or the super wealthy. The aspiring capitalist admires the wealthy and expects to be rich or richer due to the opportunities available in a competitive capitalistic society.

A list of issues, proposals and articles follows to hopefully, with input from fellow Americans, guide the nation to "a more perfect union":

Monetary Policy; Education; National Debt; Congressional Reform; Balanced Budget Amendment; Congressional Campaign Reform; Tax Reform; Congressional Benefits Reform; Energy;

Term limit; Retention of Social Security; A National Service plan; and Medicare.

The Federal government has proven its ineptitude as money-managers. We must remove the national government from the control of the alleged Social Security trust fund (trillions of dollars of an unfunded mandate has been replaced with congressional I.O.U's). Little chance of repayment is expected except by excessive taxation and increasing the age limit for benefits. Incredible mismanagement of this sort would be cause for serious prison time in the private sector.

Medicare will be financially untenable in the very near future, as well. The government has failed big time on Social Security and Medicare. The American taxpayer has been financially abused by the trillions of dollars wasted. We must, as a matter of honor, keep Social Security and Medicare for the current generation. Plans to privatize pensions and health care for future generation (preventive as well as remedial) is the optimum solution. The government cannot compete with the private sector for quality and lower costs. Monopolies have little or no incentive to advance. Research would be dead in the water. A Government monopoly with its bureaucratic waste cannot compete with private enterprise. High quality and lower costs, once again, arrives through competition, not a monopolistic government.

Promoting national budgetary solvency begins with returning so-called entitlements to the private sector. The next generation must turn to the private sector for their affordable and superior retirement and medical plans. Well-monitored private pension plans would become competitive, more efficient and less susceptible to the financial failures demonstrated by the federal government. Social Security, the federal retirement plan with its bureaucratic waste cannot compete with private enterprise. High quality and lower costs arrives through competition within the private sector as well.

A world class paradigm advancing to greater achievements

must never cease its efforts to an ever higher standard. A personal point of view will be represented in each of the aforementioned issues, proposals and articles. Your reaction and ideas are welcome. The finalized versions will be forwarded via E-Mail to each of our friends and relatives, who in turn, hopefully, will do the same. Astronomical numbers can be reached—via the internet.

The next step is to develop a platform and find candidates willing to pledge support for the planks; and, be willing to forfeit a bond or financial distress for failure to present, promote and vote for each plank. A new contract with America is in order.

A new political movement is forming. Join the millions of informed Americans who demand a restoration of a constitutional and fiscally responsible federal government. Our children and grandchildren deserve …a more perfect union. For the respect, admiration and love of a great nation– a government monopoly with its bureaucratic waste cannot compete with private enterprise.

Vote with like-thinking Americans in taking our country back at the very next election.

—Sal Terrusa
5-21-2009

FREEDOM: AN AMERICAN DYNAMIC

Out-of-control spending leading to economic servitude, in my view, is the primary question of the current presidential campaign between Senators McCain and Obama. The main issue: to be or not to be free of governmental financial abuse impacting our hard-earned income. The land of the free shall become history should unlimited taxation increasingly reduce our fellow Americans to the status of economic servitude.

Tax reform that is simple, fair and revenue sufficient (sans the grotesque governmental waste) is far past due. A balanced budget amendment failed by a single vote in the Senate during the 1994 Republican "Contract with America."

Senators McCain and Obama, how do you propose to achieve the discipline of a balanced budget amendment and the elimination of the national debt ($9 trillion and climbing) in less than a generation? Would you consider a 4% to 5% reduction per year of this grossly irresponsible debt? Our children and grandchildren are the victims of federal mismanagement and, unfortunately, a lack of citizen oversight as well. Am I being presumptuous about your interest in paying off the national debt and passing a balanced budget amendment?

Americans have not spilled their blood to be ruled by the tyranny of excessive taxation and the invasion of privacy (confiscation of property, garnishing of wages, etc.) by federal, local or any level of governmental malfeasance. Politicians must stop making promises that exceed constitutional authority and/or impose taxes we cannot afford.

Senators McCain and Obama, the electorate is eager to know what are your true specific plans regarding tax reform and a balanced budget amendment?

—Sal Terrusa

Submitted prior to the November 2008 election.
Note: It is now June 2010—still no answer re: tax reform or a balanced budget by President Obama. Candidate McCain failed to respond as well.

A PROPOSED HEALTH CARE PLAN... WILL SENIORS OPT FOR THE ICE FLOE!

It appears the Obamascare health plan may soon come out of committee and be forwarded to the House of Representatives for debate and a passage vote. The bill, if passed, may lead to Canadian type of rationing and the denial of elderly Americans for life-saving operations who have attained the age of 70 or 80. Should the proposed health care plan become law, it may be kinder to include the Alaskan Ice Floe option for the elderly. Real change may occur in the 2010 elections.

The option of luxury health insurance exists for the very wealthy and members of Congress. The politician's luxury health plan, of course, is at taxpayer's expense. Question: Why are our employees, the members of Congress, enjoying a greater privilege than their employers—the American taxpayers who pay their generous salaries and benefits?

Folks with lower incomes and non-luxury plans such as college professors like Albert Einstein and the Good Samaritan, Sister Theresa, would have been ineligible for life-saving operations. Will there be exceptions for proven geniuses? A marvelous mind would be a malicious waste. Who determines who would live and who would die?

We should not resent the smart and hard-working wealthy who can easily afford the luxury health plans—many jobs are created due to their individual and/or families' entrepreneurial successes. Political leaders like Nancy Pelosi, Harry Reid and Representatives like "Old Earmarks" Murtha, however, have demonstrated an exceptional need for political power and excessive taxation.

If Americans believed in over-taxation, we would have remained a colony of the British Empire and used our tea bags for drinking rather than dunking.

The answer to healthcare is to retire Medicare and Social Security as soon as practical and never, ever again allow big government to mismanage trillions of taxpayers' dollars. We must put a halt to federal economic ineptitude.

The private sector is the answer for lower costs and higher quality through fair but unhindered competition among medical providers and private pension plans. We can charge and punish evildoers in the private sector with heavy fines and or prison—not so with the federal government. Government monopolies have proven to be ineffective and costly.

Medicare will be broke in a very short time and the continuance of Social Security, thus far, will cost Americans trillions of dollars in unfunded liabilities. Transferring entitlement programs to the states, along with the revenues, i.e., Social Security and Medicare, and replacing gifts such as "earmarks" with low-interest, long-term loans within the next decade or so would cut the annual budget by over 50%. Further, the reduction of interest on the national debt would be lowered, as well. The next generation should be able to afford its own medical and pension plans.

The Fair Tax would permit most Americans to keep sufficient funds to pay for all of their basic expenses, including healthcare, education and retirement plans. Surrendering unreasonable income for taxes surrenders your liberty to make your own choices.

The Fair Tax is not the only alternative. We have the Flat Tax, the Ad Valorum tax and the Ron Paul version of taxation (unknown to the author). Individuals did not pay a tax in 1912 – is it possible to restore such a tax system? The author's choice is a tax on corporations and companies only, i.e., no capitation or direct tax on the individual. The tax would be based on a percentage of the Gross Domestic Product: For example 10% of the 2009 GDP would be more than 1.42 trillion dollars. I prefer 6% or less.

A successful government should monitor, regulate and carry a lower profile. Members of Congress should think of themselves as referees in a competitive contest. Can you imagine referees forming their own team and making all the rules for the league? Such a monopoly would make the game extremely dull, non-competitive and very unfair with very little incentive to improve the game. A monopolistic government competing with the automakers, banks, savings and loan institutions and insurance companies, and creating costly energy penalties (a tax), etc., is unfair, does not allow the free market to fully perform and, frankly, is extremely similar to what the former Soviet Union experienced. Did I mention the Soviets had failed?

If you agree with the article and want to send a message to our elected officials, do two things before the return of Congress in the fall: Send this E-mail or fax to your representatives (the House and the Senate). Secondly, E-mail this article to all your friends and relatives and have them do the same —the sooner, the better. Time is of the essence.

—Sal Terrusa
11-6-2009

A GREATER AMERICA

The access to an equal and fair opportunity to pursue capitalism has made the United States the most prosperous and secure nation the world has ever known. The path to collectivism i.e., socialism or communism has failed miserably in uplifting the human condition.

The power to tax is the absolute power to enslave. Over-taxation is a threat to the United States. Americans should have the right to spend most of their hard-earned money their own way; an out-of-control tax crazy central government is definitely not the answer. This happens when we fail to place limits on the governments that serve us. Enacting tax reform, a Balanced Budget Amendment, a Term limit Amendment, campaign reform, and national service are just some of the issues that have been neglected for the past 30 to 40 years. We need tax reform and abolition of the Federal Reserve NOW!

A Pre-1913 tax system would eliminate the individual from paying an income tax. Only corporations and companies paid taxes. Tax payers would not suffer the indignities and threats of paying fees, penalties, the garnishment of wages, the confiscation of property and incarceration for alleged fraud. There would be no time lost or money expended for tax preparation. April 15th would be just another day. Fearing one's government is a very poor idea. A new tax system would eliminate federal taxation bullying individual Americans.

A Fair Tax is a consumer tax. A 23% consumer tax may be necessary until we streamline the cost of running the Federal government. The Flat Tax is another possibility. How about no Federal taxes on the American people via Ron Paul? In a decade or so, local and state governments would and should receive the greater share of revenues from taxation for the general welfare. The Federal government would exist, exclusively, for national defense, international affairs, natural disasters and funding research and development. Defining a spending limit and maintaining a balanced budget amendment must be a primary goal. The U.S. Treasury would be in surplus and available for long term, low-interest rate loans to the states.

Give editors your thoughts on the following limits of governmental taxation. Let's strive for a new tax system by 2014.
EXAMPLE ONLY:
Local (city or county): 6-8%. A consumer tax.
State Government: 8-10%. A consumer tax.
Federal Government: 4-6%. For corporations and companies only.

We are currently paying between 60% and 70% of our take-home pay on all governmental taxes i.e., federal, state, property and local consumer taxes. We also pay taxes on alcohol, tobacco, utilities, recycling and far too many miscellaneous taxes to further enumerate.

A maximum of paying only 24% for all taxes would remove most governmental taxation from our backs and allow us to remain financially independent. We would have the ability to pay for our own basic needs—including healthcare and retirement plans.

ACTIONS REQUIRED:
Transfer federal funds for the general welfare to the states.
The states are in a more advantages position to know their own local needs. Any state experiencing a short fall should be able to borrow from the U.S. Treasury for a long-term, low interest rate

loan. Earmarks, gifts or grants of our tax dollars must become history, if we favor a zero-debt for the nation and a surplus in the U.S. Treasury. Loans to the states and repayment ensures economic stability.

The Federal government would still provide for the national defense but participate in a secondary role in promoting the general welfare. National defense, international affairs, natural disasters, etc. would be their primary duties—the states can handle the rest.

Diminish the federal government's bureaucracies. Double bureaucracies are wasteful, and in some areas, unconstitutional. The 10th Amendment does not permit the Federal government to establish a Federal Department of Education. An attempt to abolish or curtail the 2nd Amendment (the right to bear arms) has been attacked. Amnesty encourages more illegals.

Reforms, long past due, would make us an even greater nation. A new tax plan would eliminate over 66,000 pages from the tax code; and, abolishing the Federal Reserve would quicken the pace to economic normalcy.

A plan for enduring greatness is our mutual responsibility. Let's give our kids and grandkids something to remember us by—not an unsustainable national debt and a lower standard of living.

Use your computer to fact-check the following Federal Reserve articles: "The History of the Federal Reserve" or "The Enemies of the Federal Reserve". I am convinced you will believe the Federal Reserve System and the Income Tax must go ASAP. If you agree to a new tax code and removing the international banksters from our economic destiny—pass on this information.

The march to a greater America involves dumping the Income Tax and the Federal Reserve.

—Sal Terrusa
5-28-2010

PEOPLE POWER POLITICS AND ENERGY

Our courageous and brilliant forefathers, while fighting the British (the world's greatest military at the time) and creating a system of checks and balances to ensure the success of the new republic, warned future generations of the nature of man.

These illuminated predecessors—intelligent, knowledgeable, and honorable men—understood the predilection of men to self-interest i.e., the temptation of power to aggrandize one's self-interest at the risk of forsaking the "common welfare."

The extremely low ratings of the current Congress reflect the disappointment of the American people. Americans are very much aware of the undue influence of men and money corrupting far too many members of Congress and the Senate—we call them lobbyists. The money manipulators (The Federal Reserve) also contribute to our politicians. The checks-and-balances system has been shamefully compromised—we have become a government of, by and for the few (forgive us, Mr. Lincoln).

Let's explore the failure of Congress to resolve one of the nation's most significant problems for the last forty-plus years—energy or the lack thereof. The energy problem, we have been told, is the result of many factors: supply and demand, the petroleum cartel (aka, the OPEC pirates), the weakness of the American dollar, speculators, corrupt politicians and, last but not least, soft-headed environmentalists. All of these elements contribute to the catastrophic reality of the energy crunch.

We need more oil now and in the foreseeable future; alternative fuels and electric vehicles, etc., may take years to reach their full potential. Depending on Mid-Eastern oil places our national security at risk. The monopolistic international entity known as OPEC is not our friend (Examples: the oil embargo of 1973 and refusal to increase production of petroleum to adequate levels in 2008). Oil Profits from some Middle-Eastern countries kills and maims our troops.

Increasing our national debt to over $13 trillion dollars has compelled our government to seek and receive loans from foreign powers (China, India, Japan, etc.). Economists explain further debt depreciates the American dollar, causing us to pay more dollars to offset its weakness. Speculators, too, are hopeful that oil will continue to rise due to real or imagined shortages, which further drives up the cost of oil (some people refer to these folks as vultures). The hard-nosed environmentalists who believe it's noble to sacrifice our national security, our troops and survival to the spotted owl or some other endangered species, not to mention the seascape or other remote areas of oil-rich lands, are simply wrong. Global warming, if not a farce, has been going on for centuries. We can endure a few more years until our troops come home safely.

Environmental groups have benefitted from "violations of the green rules." Astounding! Even the greenies profit from an infraction of the environmental rules— they can legally claim a percentage of a fine for their organization. Where does the self-service end? We all want to leave a beautiful planet for our posterity—failing to survive a very dangerous nuclear world, however, may eliminate the prospect of realizing one's "posterity."

American technology will save our nation in the near future. The rest of the world will continue to depend on fossil fuel until these third world nations are able to support an infrastructure for the new technologies—that may or may not happen in this century. Time will tell.

Presidents Nixon and Carter both foresaw the need for energy independence and warned congress and the American people over three decades ago. Young Americans are apparently unaware of the Pan-Arabic oil embargo of 1973; literally hundreds of vehicles waited in line for a limited supply of gas (the embargo was intended to punish the United States—it worked).

We need to drill in spite of the Gulf's oil spill. Our energy from all sources is the key to national survival. We must make the irresponsible and reckless oil companies pay dearly for their mistakes. For your information, there are over 44,000 deep wells operating without incident. The Obama moratorium is financially harmful and questionable.

The monopolistic international purveyors of the world's oil are crushing the economies not only of the United States, but virtually every country dependent on this form of energy. We are a nation at risk and must face the challenge of a declining economy—a failing economy weakens our military, makes us vulnerable to attack, as well as a lowered standard of living. The 700 billion dollars we paid for foreign oil in 2007 would have put a lot people to work in the United States drilling for domestic oil.

The United States is facing the greatest compelling demand of the newly arrived 21st century—more independence from foreign oil until alternative fuels and a new generation of fuel efficient or electric vehicles come on line. Don't raise your hopes too high—cheap oil will still be around should the alternative fuels become more expensive. Our children and grandchildren deserve a future free from the radical rodents of economic tyranny and potential religious oppression.

A federal government directed by patriots is the key to getting the job done. Since our government is made up mostly of self-serving career politicians for the past 30-40 years who have miserably failed us on every crucial issue (in addition to the energy crisis), it is up to us, the American people, to shake up the do-nothing Congress.

American citizens, according to President Jefferson, have been encouraged to review the efficacy of government every 20-25 years and make the necessary changes according to the times. The U.S. Constitution states that we have the right and duty to retake our government through the vote or by force (if necessary). All power is given to the people; we lend that power to our representatives. We can terminate officeholders when they fail to do our bidding. The American people, thanks to our Founders, are the absolute and ultimate rulers.

The American Congress has failed; it's past time to exercise our right and duty. Let's send a strong, undeniable message: We, the American people, the absolute and ultimate rulers of our government and caretakers of our destiny, must terminate the careers of each and every incumbent at the November election. This includes incumbents we like; this is a forceful message of principle—it is not personal. Exceptions will be candidates willing to sign a contract for reforms with stiff penalties for failure.

Let's remember, *"A government big enough to give you everything you want is big enough to take away everything you have!"*
—*Thomas Jefferson*

— Sal Terrusa
2-5-2010
Revised 6-10-2010

THE NATION'S DOWNFALL: OVER-TAXATION

Re: Mr. Crisp's article "Personal responsibility needs some work". May 4, 2010.

Mr. Crisp provides us with the fact that only 22 percent of the people "Trust the government in Washington to do what is right." Further, he attacks the lack of personal responsibility of our citizens. Mr. Crisp states that consumers are 2.5 trillion dollars in debt and contributing to the nation's obesity rate.

Americans, he believes, are spending and eating too much. Mr. Crisp implies, seemingly, that "Big Government" is needed due to the out-of-control habits of its citizens. The implication has some merit. I agree with Mr. Crisp that personal responsibility may be a part of the problem but for a different reason.

Mr. Crisp said, "Perhaps government can become too big; if it does, it should be taken in hand." Mr. Crisp, out of fairness, the Tea Party movement has been screaming to the high heavens that the government IS too big. The government has been too big since the era of President Wilson. Mr. Wilson sold out the United States to a cartel of international bankers who fallaciously referred to themselves as the Federal Reserve. The Federal Reserve is a private corporation of international bankers who are in business to make a profit for themselves and their mostly foreign shareholders—not the American taxpayer.

The 1913 Income Tax code made it possible to tax anything

that is static or dynamic. Americans are and have been the victims of "legal larceny" due the Federal Reserve Act and the arrival of the Income Tax Amendment both in the year of our lord, 1913. It took a while to introduce the main topic, "Over Taxation."

Bigger government, as a possible solution, is ludicrous! Social Security is 56 trillion dollars in debt due to unfunded liabilities. Medicare can be sustained for only a few more years at the present rate of growth. The new healthcare bill is financially questionable. The national debt is over 13 trillion dollars and growing. A bloated government wastes our tax dollars. The federal government, the king of waste, sets a very poor example for the people it is suppose to serve. The balancing of national budgets has been ignored—unlike what most American families do to balance their budgets. President Jackson, incidentally, was the only president in history to achieve a zero debt for the nation.

The Federal Government serves as a role model to be avoided.

Members of congress who receive campaign funds from bankers have colluded to compel Americans to use credit cards due to over-taxation. With less take-home pay citizens must resort to credit cards and loans to meet their basic needs. The winners are the bankers and all financial institutions that collect interest monthly on the credit cards and loans. The items purchased, after combining the principal and interest paid, triples and sometimes quadruples the original cost of an item.

Mr. Crisp and I agree that the American people must physically exercise (by running, not trotting to the nearest poll booths) during the November elections of 2010 and 2012. Physical fitness, avoiding credit card purchases and high interest loans by paying cash must be American goals. Over-taxation leading to less take-home pay must be reversed. Lower taxes and more take-home pay is the answer. We desperately need a new tax system that is fair, simple and adequate. The pre-1913 tax code must be restored. The states, however, must assume Social Security and Medicare responsibilities (along with the revenues). Privitization must evolve with the next generation.

Americans will be a part of the problem if they fail to exercise their responsibility to vote. Voting for lower taxes and more take-home pay would permit sufficient funds to purchase more nutritious food, a gym membership and paying cash for large appliances and smaller fuel-efficient cars. Bankers and financial institutions would not suffer the loss of profits from less interest earned. Increased activity would more than suffice for the lost interest. The good news: A win-win situation.

Better news: We, the people, would be out of the recession much sooner.

—Sal Terrusa
5-7-2010

AN ENLIGHTENED CIVILIZATION
A PATH TO WORLD PEACE

The advance of nuclear proliferation into the arsenals of our enemies places the entire world at risk. An enlightened civilization of the future may do away with war and armies. In the present time, it is our destiny to survive an imperfect world— with the hopeful goal of making it a safer place— if we can. The greatest military force in modern history may give our nation the time needed to seek a path to world peace.

Peace through strength is far more enduring than peace through appeasement.

Common sense dictates the greater military should be at our disposal. Peace in our time relies on the balance of military power among opposing forces. The world needs time to develop a lasting peace through the world-wide intellectual abhorrence and rejection of war as the ultimate solution—before it's too late.

The U.S. military is overextended. We need the unity and strength of all the American people to do our duty as civilians as well as members of the military to fully protect the nation. An expanded military is immeasurably most effective with total civilian support (as was demonstrated in WWII).

Once a war had been thrust upon us or after Congress had declared war, anti-war movements are irrational, dangerous, and, frankly, an act of selfishness and/or cowardice by some of our fellow citizens. The disturbing attitude of "Let G.I. Joe or Jane protect my rights, and to hell with taking my turn in the trenches" defies the American sense of fair play and duty.

Public dissenters of an armed conflict must weigh their open dissent against how many soldiers will lose their lives unnecessarily by giving hope to the enemy. Conscientious objectors, in war-time, have the option of volunteering for the medical corp. The greatest promise for peace is to be highly prepared for war—more so than a potential foe. An enemy must believe a war with the United States is not only unwinnable but unthinkable.

Expanding the military with the offer of educational benefits provides many economic and national security benefits for the future as well as the present. Providing the higher education benefits through a national service plan (similar but superior to WWII's GI bill) would promote a prosperous and more secure nation.

A warning: A plan for national service (i.e., military, Peace Corps, etc.), must be implemented immediately—the world is too unstable and treacherous a place to tolerate a delay. Rationale: three to four tours of duty by military personnel implies we are lacking in troop strength, not only for Iraq and Afghanistan, but contingency forces available for other possible confrontations. Our enemies, as well as our allies, are very much aware of these inadequate troop levels.

The Russian bear is growling and needs to be tamed; let's make Russia a partner in capitalism and appreciate their need for a sense of security among nations. Millions of Russians died in WWII fighting the Nazis (they have a right to be paranoid). Let's keep Russia as an ally or, at least, neutralized by a show of force. North Korea requires world-wide pressure to confront their belligerence. Dictatorships must be consistently challenged for military adventurism. Faithful allies must be a part of the peace-keeping duties. Fairness requires sharing the duties of peace-keeping among nations.

During WWII, very few Americans rejected the draft or failed to support the troops or their leaders. If they had, we may have become bilingual, speaking Japanese and/or German. Consider the following: "How's your Arabic? Do radical Islamic terrorists offer you a choice?" Does the advance of civilization use women and children as human shields in combat? Have we forgotten 9/11 so soon?

In wars past, millions of Americans have been maimed—others have made the ultimate sacrifice to keep us free. No true conscionable American should have a free ride—even Canadians have deported our deserters. Canadians have changed their policy of giving refuge to U.S. deserters. Young Canadian soldiers are dying in Afghanistan along with young American soldiers; could that be the reason for the policy change?

A National Service Plan for Volunteers may make the draft unnecessary. The inducement of educational benefits for these volunteers would promote an all-volunteer military or an opportunity for civil service i.e., the Peace Corp, AmeriCorps, National Park Service, Etc.

A draft would occur only in an all out war for survival.

—Sal Terrusa
(modified) 5-20-2010

SARAH PALIN: 2012?

Citizen Sarah Palin was discovered using a few words on the palm of her hand to recall, obviously, the salient points of her presentation. Sarah demonstrated she could speak "off the cuff" with only a few words to keep her on point. On nationwide television, it takes confidence, skill and an outstanding memory to succeed. She received wild applause eleven times during her speech. President Barack Obama, we know, has used teleprompters to read many of his lengthy speeches. The president is a very bright man and has proven his retentive memory at town meetings. For citizens who have watched the president always using a teleprompter, however, may find his performance suspect. The president, we know, is a busy executive and doesn't always have the time or luxury of writing and/or memorizing his own speeches.

A question has arisen multiple times—is Sarah ready to be President of the United States? Would I vote, today, for Sarah Palin to be President of the United States?

The answer is no.

Mrs. Palin has written a highly successful book and is in great demand as a speaker for millions of conservative Americans who see her as a model of rugged individualism and symbolic of the American spirit. Mrs. Palin may become a very wealthy woman in the very near future. Should Sarah use this new found wealth to give her the time to study national and international issues and become a knowledgeable candidate for the

Presidency in 2012—who knows what might happen? Sarah has exhibited common sense, compassion, humor and, most importantly, character. We need a true leader who we can trust and doesn't speak with a bi-furcated tongue.

I may vote for a more knowledgeable and a continually growing Sarah Palin who definitely possesses the character we have come to expect in our Commander-in-Chiefs—time will tell. A fact: I am pulling for all the Sarah Palins we have in our great country. Much can happen in less than three years before 2012.

—Sal Terrusa
5-24-10

IS THE FEDERAL RESERVE NECESSARY?

Sam Donaldson, moderator of a. T.V. show, on 6/7/2010 posed the following question to Ben Bernanke, President of the controversial Federal Reserve: "How important is the Federal Reserve?" Bernanke's response: "Every nation needs a central bank. There are over 180 nations in the world." Mr. Bernanke, it seems, was implying that all nations could not survive without a central bank (a central bank is a larger bank with greater assumed assets and able to lend funds to lower level banks at a discount). Example: a wholesaler who offers discounted money to retailers.

The seventh president of the United States, Andrew Jackson, terminated the services of a central bank and over 700 hundred of its suspected federal employees. The result: It is the first and only time that a president of the United States left office without incurring debt. The United States has flourished quite well and often without a central bank at the helm. President Jackson returned the financial duties to its constitutionally endowed U.S. Treasury (Article1, Section 8).

The fallaciously named Federal Reserve System is a private cartel of International bankers. The name, Federal Reserve, was used to conceal the fact that the cartel had taken over the constitutional function of the United States Treasury. These international bankers have formed a trust or a monopoly similar to the oil cartel known as OPEC (Organization of Petroleum Exporting Countries). The Federal Reserve uses its profits to serve itself and its shareholders. It is a private corporation and does not have the American taxpayer as its primary fiduciary responsibility. The Federal Reserve has its shareholders to consider and bank profits. These money manipulators print our currency and fix interest rates without fear of competition among other lesser banks. Their profits are not taxed by the U.S. government.

The immoral practice of fractional banking is a banking custom of printing more money than it actually has supportive commodities in its possession such as gold or silver, etc. If ordinary citizens were printing this form of insupportable money—they would be jailed for counterfeiting. The practice of fractional banking should be recognized as outside of the law.

Borrowing fiat money, without restraint, makes it virtually impossible to rid ourselves of the national debt. The 2010 national debt is more than 13 trillion dollars and climbing. We must reinstitute the constitutional provision of having the United States Treasury resume its duties of printing our own currency and the setting of interest rates as well as receiving the profits from judicious loans extended to borrowers.

Caution: Corruption shall always be a problem in government. The U.S. Treasury and all governmental bureaucracies must still be strictly monitored with above-reproach regulators, incentivized whistle blowers and undercover operators. President Reagan believed, with significant treaties and transactions, we must "Trust but verify".

The Federal Reserve contributes to the campaigns and re-elections of our public officials which perpetuates a class of career politicians (to the dismay of our Founders). A Term limit would replace parasitical career politicians with patriotic officeholders. That is a subject for another article.

Abolishing the alleged Federal Reserve and the unfair, inadequate, unnecessarily punitive and purposely complicated Income Tax (more than 66,000 pages) are the keys to a more secure and prosperous nation. The Federal Reserve Act and the Income Tax Amendment arrived in the same year-1913. The greedy feds wanted more taxation and the means to collect the increased taxation (the IRS was created).

We must reinstitute the U.S. Treasury to print our currency and set interest rates and a new tax plan strictly limited to a percentage of the GDP (Gross Domestic Product). These reforms, alone, would free us from the financial slave-master relationship with the alleged Federal Reserve and a possible life of serfdom. Americans would be less victimized by some of the greediest banksters and most corrupt politicians on the planet

—Sal Terrusa
6-10-2010

THE BLOW OUT!

The petroleum industry is guilty in failing to successfully research and advance safer drilling methodologies in deep water. The United States government may have irresponsibly practiced improper supervision and monitoring. Thousands of successful deep-water wells, however, are functioning today without serious notoriety. An independent investigation must provide some urgent answers for the BP blowout.

Engineers and scientists have demonstrated successful ways to rapidly clean-up oil spills and preserve the oil at the same time. These new inventions must be provided in greater numbers to meet the massive oil spill in the Gulf of Mexico without further delay. It matters not who is responsible at this time – we must stop the catastrophe first. The President, eventually, must give a straight answer as to why he did not accept the help of several nations at the beginning of the spill. The clean-up during the very first days may have mitigated the damage to the environment.

The world's population will explode in the next 50 years or so. Energy of all kinds will be needed to meet the increased demands. Oil will be with us for at least a century unless we blow ourselves up in a nuclear conflagration. Oil companies are expanding, not retreating, in spite of the call for alternative fuels. Oil will still be the fuel of choice if it is cheaper than alternative fuels.

The Cap and Trade movement to reduce carbon emissions requires that all polluting-nations cooperate. All oil-producing nations will not cooperate because it is not in their best interest to lose the grandiose profits from selling their oil to 180 oil-starved nations and meeting their own energy needs. Cap and Trade is another term for increased taxation. Why would the United States government increase your taxes in a dire economy? Politicians are always suspect when it comes to increasing our taxes. Scientists are divided on carbon emissions. If you trust our current politicians then go ahead—give the rest of your paycheck to an already over-sized and wasteful government.

The President's moratorium on oil places the embattled oil-workers and the entire United States economy in an unnecessary precarious circumstance. Thousands will lose their jobs, oil and gas prices will increase and the government will have less revenue due to the failed businesses. Repealing the moratorium is risky. In any event, we cannot afford the moratorium—we must continue to drill and remain tough in the oil business. Thousand of deep water wells, as you know, are functioning without incident. China, India, Russia, Venezuela, Brazil and the OPEC nations need oil to survive—so does the United States. We must become a nation independent of foreign oil.

Environmentalists, it is past time to observe the need for Americans to invade the oil markets and reduce the profits from the oil our enemies use to kill and maim our troops. Saving our loved ones in the service of our country comes first. Humankind must take precedence over other species and the various environmental concerns. Just as there is no crying in baseball—there should be no crying in keeping oil in the future mix of energy as the world's population mushrooms towards the 20 billion mark or more before the end of the century. Some scientist say that oil is a finite substance and injurious to our health. Some scientists believe we can keep oil under control with alternative fuels. Time will tell. In the interim, you may want to check with your broker as the price of oil begins to soar.

—Sal Terrusa
6-25-2010

WHO ARE THE TEA PARTY FOLLOWERS?

Citizens supporting the Tea Party goals have gained the attention of millions of their fellow Americans. The movement is nationwide. It's no wonder! The goals appeal to the common sense of constitutionally enlightened Americans. Who can argue with respecting constitutional limitations; regaining fiscal responsibility and favoring free-market capitalism? Independents, Republicans and Democrats have swelled the numbers desiring a return to proven American principles. Members of Congress who ignore our brilliant founders are arrogant, ignorant, constitutionally misinformed, and corrupt or power hungry. Please fill-in any categories I may have missed. American financial and political freedom is at risk—it's time to take back the promise of America— that is, equal opportunity for all and personal freedoms.

Re: Constitutional Limitations—the constitution provided for the U.S. Treasury to print our own currency and establish the interest rates. (Article 1, Section 8). In 1913, the Federal Reserve Act was passed which usurped the duties of the U.S. Treasury. The financial status of the United States has been in chaos ever since. The Federal Reserve is a private corporation of international bankers. The use of the word "Federal" was used to conceal its true identity. The "Fed" is a cartel or monopoly also known as a central bank. Its primary purpose is earning profits for the bank and its mostly foreign shareholders. Its legal fiduciary duty is to the shareholders and not the American taxpayers. The Great Depression and the recent financial crises are the result of the Federal Reserve's action or inaction—the choice is yours. The "Feds" in conjunction with self-serving legislators have driven our federal debt to more than 13 trillion dollars. There is a two step procedure to eliminate the debt. Step number one—abolish the Federal Reserve or activate Executive Order 11110. Either action would put the Federal Reserve out of business. Step number two—suggestions for eliminating the national debt are revealed in the next paragraph.

Re: Fiscal Responsibility—we can repay the 13 trillion dollars national debt with fiat money—the same kind of money that the "Feds" loaned to us. Abe Lincoln used "greenbacks" to pay for the Civil War to avoid the more than 30% interest on the loans the central banks had planned to charge the North. All countries have the right to create their own currency. The current and future assets of a nation support its currency. Our fiat money would be backed by the tremendous mineral wealth we have stored underground in the U.S. and Alaska.

The "Feds" have never been audited. Without an audit, monopoly money may have more value. We don't need to audit the "Feds"—we need to terminate the "Feds". Further, the use of the word "federal" was a fraud perpetrated on the American people. A basis for a criminal and or a civil suit may be in order.

The Income Tax must be repealed. At the present time, there is no limit to what the federal government would or could charge its citizens within the current tax system. You could lose all your property and or financial assets. Bankruptcy due to non-payment of taxes is a common occurrence. Financial uncertainty is occurring for more than 9.5% of the unemployed within the American work force. We must limit Federal government taxation by having corporations and companies pay a fixed amount of the GDP (Gross Domestic Product). A capitation tax was unconstitutional in 1912. The individual did not pay an income tax. Only corporations and companies paid taxes before 1913. Returning to a Pre-1913 tax code optimizes our liberties.

Extravagant government waste and double bureaucracies have crippled our economy. Allowing the States to take a larger share of the Common Welfare such as Social Security and Medicare along with the revenues makes sense. The Federal government has grossly mishandled financial matters. A new Tax System will return more than 40% of one's take-home pay. Citizens could afford the same pension and medical plans members of Congress are enjoying tody. The Federal government must live within its means.

National defense and international affairs must be its priorities. Wars must involve the peoples' will for full support. During war-time, sell war bonds, if necessary.

We must never allow Congress to spend money we don't have. An emergency fund must be created and replenished as needed.

Re: Free markets or Capitalism—maintaining a fair playing field in the business world requires trusted regulators. Anti-Trust laws must be enforced. Since regulators have been corrupted in the past, the FBI must monitor regulators. Should the FBI fail—our last line of defense may have to be the nation's Eagle Scouts—character counts. The competition inherent in capitalism assures higher quality and lower prices for all products and services. Socialism and Communism inhibits the pursuit for excellence. Marxism relies on other peoples' money—perhaps, your own. Join a Tea Party to restore American freedoms.

—Sal Terrusa
7-4-2010

KNOW YOUR RIGHTS
Re: Miriam Albert's piece about "Leaving Words Out"

Miriam Albert inferred only the "militia" had the right to bear arms. The Founders of the constitution covered all bases by using the word unalienable or inalienable rights, if you prefer.

Further, the 10th Amendment stated that which is not specifically expressed (written) in the constitution is a right belonging to the state or to the people. The right of self-defense for yourself or the protection of your family is an inalienable right. The 10th Amendment supports that right. So much for the paper work. It is a matter of insanity to believe the constitution or any other document could take away your right to defend yourself and your loved ones with any kind of weapon available—be it a baseball bat, a kitchen knife, a Saturday night special, a shotgun, an assault weapon or an artillery piece (in the event of a tyrannical take-over of the government).

In the city of Los Angeles, it takes an average of ten and one-half minutes to respond to a 911 call. By that time, without the inalienable right to bear arms and the support of the 10th Amendment, you and your entire family may be at the mercy of a criminal with robbery, rape or murder on his mind. The law of self-defense to protect life is in the books regardless of the type of weapon used. If the police can't help by coming to your rescue in time—a potential victim is not going to wait for the "militia" to show up.

Still not convinced? The natural law of the jungle is still in existence. Animals will fight to the death against predators or choose to run. Mama bear, however, would never abandon her cubs.

Finally, if you surrender your second Amendment rights, you may doom your posterity to a tyrannical government. Freedom would be a faint memory after a generation or two. Crime rose by 40% in England after banning guns.

—Sal Terrusa
7-7-2010

A "CHANGE" FOR THE BETTER?

President Obama must search the deepest recesses of his mind if he believes the American people will swallow his socializing political agenda. If you cannot accept the fact that President Obama is a collectivist then you haven't been paying attention to his actions. President Obama desires to have the folks ultimately and completely controlled by the federal government. King Obama may be able to lop off some heads soon without the 'Damn Constitution!' getting in his way.

Taxing the shirt off your back translates to being dependent on the government for all of your needs: food, clothing, transportation, utilities, phones, computer, education, entertainment, transportation, health and pension expenditures. Oops! I almost forgot your taxes i.e., federal, state, property and consumer taxes in addition to the hidden taxes in items such as alcohol, tobacco, gas, recycling and countless others that would have to be paid. We already have food stamps. The government believes it has the ability to make all your economic decisions providing you surrender your entire paycheck to the Feds. So far it's more than 60% of your take home pay (including all the aforementioned items). Will the Feds try for more of your take-home pay?

You can't afford to pay your taxes? Not to worry! Your more affluent neighbors and small business owners will help you out as soon as they pay for their expenses-providing they haven't used up all their take-home pay or profits, respectively.

When neighbors go broke and small businesses go out of business for failure to pay their taxes, you can count on the government to come to the rescue. Really! The Obama administration wants business under the control of federal regulators; he claims otherwise but more than 60% of the private sector has shifted to federal government control in the last 18 months. It was less than 40% before he took office. The more bankruptcies mean the unemployed will have to depend on government. The more dependant citizens become, the larger the role of a growing government. More bureaucrats means more taxation and the cycle continues until every American wonders if they will be next on the growing breadlines. More taxation bloats the federal government and leaves little take-home pay for our fellow Americans.

The "humanitarians" in Washington D.C. need a break from finding new ways to spend our money. Let's keep more of our money and take responsibility for paying our own debts. We need to cut out the middle man - the irresponsible, wasteful and corrupt federal government. An 11% approval rating for congress says it all.

A paraphrase with a twist follows: Ask not what you can do for yourself but what you can do for the government to live within its means - as we do.

On the other hand, as the Socialists run out of other peoples' money, why not consider the free market of the early 1900's when we were economically way ahead of the rest of the world? The solution is relatively simple. Reduce government expenses in half by cutting the extreme waste report by Glen Beck's research team; or pay all government workers and elected officials a minimum wage until the economy recovers. Wouldn't that light a fire under our slow-moving politicians!? Demanding a balanced budget and limited taxation is a better idea.

Americans must reject any and all forms of collectivism such as Socialism or Communism. Most, if not all, international bankers and powerful industrialists do not choose to engage in competition. Greedy world class bankers, like the Federal Reserve, and some equally corrupt oil barons, like OPEC, prefer a world where competition is annihilated in favor of a system of monopolies. The Federal Reserve is a cartel or monopoly of international bankers.

The opportunity to achieve economic success for ambitiously aspiring Americans, as is possible under capitalism, is becoming a thing of the past. Out-of-control taxation would force Americans to be dependent on an eternally corrupt federal government with little or no chance to regain what used to be our money. Our money and our freedom are rapidly disappearing.

"Give me liberty or give me death." The Revolutionary war cry that may rise, once again, to preserve America's last best hope for freedom. It is far better to stop excessive-taxation nonsense at the ballot box this coming November. We need to abolish the greatest financial evil that has ever enslaved Americans since 1913 — the Federal Reserve. Next, we need a new tax system based on a percentage of the Gross Domestic Product (GDP). The income tax must go, along with the IRS. The individual must resume a Pre-1913 status. The individuals did not pay a tax in 1913 - only corporations and companies paid taxes. It was against the constitution for an individual to pay a capitation tax. A new tax system can and must be enacted.

What can we expect from Socialism? A two-tier social system would evolve: the extremely wealthy and those who would serve the extremely wealthy. Wake up American! Our kids deserve better.

—Sal Terrusa 7-10-2010
Revised: 8-5-2010

"WHERE LAW ENDS, TYRANNY BEGINS."

—William Pitt

The "unconstitutional" Federal Department of Education has violated the 10th Amendment and usurped the power and funds that belong exclusively to the states or to the people.

Congress has voted to spend 26 billion dollars to save the jobs of 140,000 teachers. Congress has no constitutional right to be involved with the education of our children or their teachers—an exception may be the military academies. The military academies would and should be funded by the defense department's budget.

The budget for the current Federal Department of Education is $162.3 billion dollars – A sum that should remain with the states or the people. The breakdown: $63.7 billion in FY 2010 as discretionary spending and $98.6 billion in discretionary spending provided under the American Recovery and Investment Act of 2009.

The impact on the state of California follows: California with 12.5% of the nation's population would receive $3,250,000 billion dollars of the $26 billion dollars offered by the feds. If the 10th Amendment were respected by members of Congress and the misappropriated funds were returned to the states—Californians would receive 12.5% of $162.3 billion dollars or more than

$20.2 billion dollars (which would cover California's entire educational shortfall and much of the remaining balance of the state's deficit).

California would have eliminated virtually its entire debt for 2010. How many more states would have a balanced budget if the "feds" surrendered its unconstitutional behavior by hoarding our tax dollars?

More importantly, the central or federal government would not have the opportunity to propagandize or brainwash our children. We fought a Revolutionary war to rid ourselves of the tyrant, King George III. Education must be the exclusive province of the states or the people to avoid the opportunity for a rising or future tyranny.

If a state needs funds to improve their educational programs or projects—allow the U.S. Treasury to extend long term and low interest rate loans instead of outright grants or gifts. We must stop draining the Treasury. Taking money away from one state and then giving it to another is redistribution of wealth. Robbing Peter to pay Paul must be unacceptable behavior in the U.S. Congress as it is in the private sector.

We seem powerless to control outrageous and criminal-like congressional spending. Members of Congress are spending our tax dollars as if it were their own personal money. All personal income is taxed under our current system. The current option is to vote them out of office. The press must do its watchdog duty and publish the voting records of all members of Congress prior to the November elections. We still have the internet if the press should continue to fail us.

—Sal Terrusa

THE CHALLENGE OF CAPITALISM

Capitalism has made the United States the wealthiest and most envied of nations. Maintaining the integrity of capitalism is a daunting challenge.

The current giants of some banking, financial institutions, industry and corrupt political officials, unfortunately, have joined to prevent the rise of future competitors. Monopolies and cartels are the death of capitalism which relies on competition for the greater good of consumers. Anti-trust laws, thus far, have been ineffective. The character of future regulators must be beyond reproach. The F.B.I. and state officials must screen and monitor regulators much more effectively.

Excessive over-taxation by the government is bad news for entrepreneurs as well as its citizens. The failure of new enterprises to succeed is a threat, not only to the entrepreneur, but the economic health of American citizens. Prices will rise and quality will suffer without competition.

The nefarious corruption of high U.S. government officials due to the power and influence of money (contributions or bribes, etc.) screams for a fairer system of campaigning. Public funding and access to T.V. and public radio for less affluent candidates may level the playing field. It is unfair and un-American to keep teachers and firemen, etc. from campaigning because of prohibitive sums of money required for campaigning.

Communism and Socialism have failed all over the world. Communists and Socialists love a weakened American economy.

The Socialist believes it provides an opportunity for Socialism to override Capitalism. Socialism robs Peter to pay Paul. When Peter runs out of money we have predictable failure. Socialism is a two-tier system: Those who rule and those who serve the rulers. Collectivists are sneaky—after a few generations have passed, the newest generation will not be able to recall the benefits of individual freedoms their grandparents or parents had lost.

In America, the people have the constitutional power to determine who will be their leaders and to remove inefficient or corrupt elected officials. Many incumbents may not be with us in the near future.

World- wide fair competition is the answer to prosperity for the optimum number of people on the planet. May Americans continue to set a prosperous pace for global competition.

Vote for candidates unafraid to meet national and global challenges.

—Sal Terrusa

THE INTOLERABLE ACTS OF THE 21ST CENTURY

The citizens of the United States must claim the exclusive right to control their own financial destiny. The president, congress and the foreign bank known, fallaciously, as the Federal Reserve have failed the American People. Exploding the national debt by over-taxation and out-of-control spending must be immediately confronted and terminated.

We must also remove the Federal Reserve from our shores. The Federal Reserve is a private corporation of international bankers -it is not an entity of the U.S. Government. The majority of shareholders are foreigners. The fiduciary duty of the so-called Federal Reserve is to these foreign shareholders-not the American taxpayer. Google the Federal Reserve to authenticate the aforementioned statement.

A new amendment, which would give the American people the exclusive right to determine the rate of taxation by way of the referendum, is proposed. Americans must never again become vulnerable to excessive taxation and exorbitant waste by a federal government under the control of self-serving elected officials and a foreign group of bankers.

Further, a new tax code must be introduced. We may need to re-enact the Ad Valorum tax that existed in 1912 The Ad Valorum Tax of 1912 was imposed on corporations and companies only-not the individual. It was contrary to the constitution, under this particular tax plan, to impose a capitation tax on the individual. Most Americans enjoyed the greater income from their labors which allowed them to not only meet their basic needs but also save and exercise the opportunity to compete in the business world. Great fortunes, in many instances, were amassed due to a government that was not over-sized or wasteful. The American worker would have more than 40% to 50% in their take-home pay under the Ad Valorum Tax system. Americans would enjoy the same medical and retirement benefits of congress.

An alternative Business Tax based on the 2010. GDP (Gross Domestic Product) would yield more than $840 billion dollars (almost twice the annual budget of the early part of the century).

Three giant steps to a greater America follow:

1. Enact an alternative Business Tax at 6% of the GDP and terminate the complex, inadequate, unfair and punitive 16th Amendment (the Income Tax).

2. Re-institute the U.S. Treasury for all of our banking needs under Article 1. Section 8 of the original constitution. Repeal the Federal Reserve Act of 1913 and dump the foreigners.

3. Impose a single term limit on a member of the House for 4 years and a single term limit of 6 years for a senator. Retain, however, the current term limits for the presidency. An outstanding presidential candidate and potential world leader is a rarity and a second term should be available in this instance.

The Founders fought a war to dismiss a ruling class of elitist. They understood citizen- legislators were capable of governance and should share these duties by rotating the responsibility with fellow Americans. Removing career politicians, not unlike changing baby diapers frequently, should occur often and for the same reason.

—Sal Terrusa

A "MORATORIUM" ON EARMARKS!?

Senator Orrin Hatch, incredulously, stated on Fox TV this past week (11/10/10) that we need a two year "moratorium" on earmarks. Earmarks are unconstitutional, extremely unfair, and unlimited extravagance. The nation is on the verge of bankruptcy largely due to irresponsible federal spending of which "earmarks" is a significant part of the problem—in spite of the naysayers.

Many of our greatest presidents declared the giving away of "free" public money for parochial purposes was *unconstitutional* and for good reason. The following excerpts by Julie Kesselman are from an article which appeared on Townhall.com on February 22nd:

"The idea of funneling federal funds to *specific local projects* originally came from Congressman John C. Calhoun, when he proposed the Bonus Bill of 1817 to construct highways linking the East and South of the United States to its Western frontier (referred to as "internal improvements"). Calhoun wanted to use the earnings bonus from the Second Bank of the United States specifically for this program, arguing that the General Welfare and Post Roads clauses of the United States Constitution allowed for it.

Without speaking to its merits, President James Madison vetoed the bill as unconstitutional. He explains his reasoning to

Congress in his veto message:

"*Having considered the bill ... I am constrained by the insuperable difficulty I feel in reconciling this bill with the Constitution of the United States. ... The legislative powers vested in Congress are specified ... in the ... Constitution, and it does not appear that the power proposed to be exercised by the bill is among the enumerated powers. ...*"

And regarding the General Welfare Clause, Madison responds:

"*Such a view of the Constitution would have the effect of giving to Congress a general power of legislation instead of the defined and limited one hitherto understood to belong to them, the terms 'common defense and general welfare' embracing every object and act within the purview of a legislative trust.*"

Directly from the horse's mouth, ladies and gentlemen: earmarking is not an enumerated power of Congress. Nor is it written in stone anywhere, as the Honorable J. Denny Hastert seems to think; that is, earmarking is "what members do" or that members are best positioned to know where to put a "red light in their district" (urban planners in state and local governments are probably better adept to determine the position of traffic lights than the 20-something staffers piling on the earmarks in DC)."

The following quote is by Tom Finnegan-updated March 7, 2007 from Needed Reforms:

"For much of the nation's history, constitutional objections from members of Congress, the president, and state legislatures were effective in limiting parochial spending.

The First Congress rejected a bill to loan money to a glass manufacturer after several members challenged the constitutionality of the proposal. In a debate during the Second Congress over a bill to pay a bounty to New England cod fisherman, Rep. Hugh Williamson of South Carolina argued that it was unconstitutional "to gratify one part of the Union by oppressing the other ... destroy this barrier; and, it is not a few fishermen that will enter, but all manner of persons; people of every trade and occupation may enter in at the breach, until they have eaten up the bread of our children."

Earmarks are extremely unfair because it gives the incumbent virtually millions of dollars to return projects, wanted or unwanted, to his or her congressional district assuring re-election; an unfair competitive barrier for a candidate challenging an incumbent. Robbing one congressional district to enhance another is likened to grand theft; and, contrary to the specific and required limitations of the U.S. Constitution.

Earmarks are extravagant and wasteful because, over the past decade, they have contributed to the nation's indebtedness of more than thirteen trillion dollars—with no relief in sight. The knowledgeable "unconstitutional" wasting of the people's money is treacherous and bordering on treason—public officials have sworn to uphold the constitution. Not abuse it.

A commonsense solution would be to borrow the formerly "free" money and pay it back over a long term and at a low interest rate. If they had to pay for the requested earmarks, they may reconsider the loan. In any event, the incumbents must stop the unfair and unconstitutional draining of the U.S. Treasury. Both sides of the so-called aisle are participants in this illegal act. You can vote them out in 2012 or recall them even sooner. We need to fill the coffers of the U.S. treasury for our children and grandchildren, not the pockets' of self-serving parasitic politicians.

Patriots will vote to *abolish earmarks* in favor of long term, low interest rate loans preserving the surplus in the U.S. Treasury.

Corrupt incumbents will maintain the *unconstitutional and financially reckless* status quo to gain an advantage for re-election.

The 2009 total comes to 11,914 earmarks at a *cost of $28.9 billion*. This represents the second most earmarks-and the second highest cost-in American history. In a generation, indexed for inflation, more than a trillion dollars will have been spent, unnecessarily.

—Sal Terrusa

PART 3

Part 3
ARTICLES BY OTHERS
Introduction

Many significant ideas and invaluable information by several authors provided the impetus for Mr. Terrusa's Chapters and Articles in this book. Access to these credible authors and their subject matter is essential to a comprehensive understanding of the issues of our times. The way forward to the on-going American political experiment would be sustained by an informed electorate.

The imperfection of mankind has been well established. Evaluating the merits of men therefore becomes a matter of relativity. For example: the founders of the United States were honorable mental giants. We must, by necessity, become aware of the corruptive mental midgets of our times. Your vote will assist in compelling these ex-congressional members to search for new jobs they can "honestly" handle. It's the American Way.

Socialism has failed in the Soviet Union, Great Britain, Europe and Asia. Collectivists: Get over it!

Free market capitalism properly and fairly regulated would empower and sustain the world's greatest economic system. The corrupt oil trust such as OPEC or greedy international banking monopolies known as the Federal Reserve or the IMF (the International Monetary Fund) must be marginalized, if not eliminated.

Global governments such as the United Nations must not be allowed to impair national sovereignty. These world institutions desire power which comes with the ability to tax without limitation. They may request only one percent in the beginning and then the rest of your hard-earned labors once the flood gates have been opened. The American Income tax began with only one percent in 1913 for the very rich. We all know what happened to that plan.

Until all Americans become informed as to the forces impairing the United States from remaining the world's greatest nation, we shall become the continued victims of the world's greediest people, the International bankers.

1938 AUSTRIA
By Kitty Werthmann
Reprinted by Permission

Kitty Werthmann telling her story:
What I am about to tell you are some things you've probably never heard or will ever read in history books. I believe that I am an eyewitness to history. I cannot tell you that Hitler took Austria by tanks and guns; it would distort history. We elected him by a landslide - 98% of the vote. I've never read that in any American publications. Everyone thinks that Hitler just rolled in with his tanks and took Austria by force. In 1938, Austria was in deep Depression. Nearly one-third of our work force was unemployed. We had 25% inflation and 25% bank loan interest rates. Farmers and business people were declaring bankruptcy daily. Young people were going from house to house begging for food. Not that they didn't want to work; there simply weren't any jobs. My mother was a Christian woman and believed in helping people in need. Every day we cooked a big kettle of soup and baked bread to feed those poor, hungry people —about 30 daily. The Communist Party and the National Socialist Party were fighting each other. Blocks and blocks of cities like Vienna, Linz, and Graz were destroyed. The people became desperate and petitioned the government to let them decide what kind of government they wanted. We looked to our neighbor on the north, Germany, where Hitler had been in power since 1933. We had been told that they didn't have unemployment or crime,

and they had a high standard of living. Nothing was ever said about persecution of any group — Jewish or otherwise. We were led to believe that everyone was happy. We wanted the same way of life in Austria. We were promised that a vote for Hitler would mean the end of unemployment and help for the family. Hitler also said that businesses would be assisted, and farmers would get their farms back. Ninety-eight percent of the population voted to annex Austria to Germany and have Hitler for our ruler. We were overjoyed, and for three days we danced in the streets and had candlelight parades. The new government opened up big field kitchens and everyone was fed.

After the election, German officials were appointed, and like a miracle, we suddenly had law and order. Three or four weeks later, everyone was employed. The government made sure that a lot of work was created through the Public Work Service. Hitler decided we should have equal rights for women. Before this, it was a custom that married Austrian women did not work outside the home. An able-bodied husband would be looked down on if he couldn't support his family. Many women in the teaching profession were elated that they could retain the jobs they previously had been required to give up for marriage.

HITLER TARGETS EDUCATION, ELIMINATES RELIGIOUS INSTRUCTION FOR CHILDREN

Our education was nationalized. I attended a very good public school. The population was predominantly Catholic, so we had religion in our schools. The day we elected Hitler (March 13, 1938), I walked into my schoolroom to find the crucifix replaced by Hitler's picture hanging next to a Nazi flag. Our teacher, a very devout woman, stood up and told the class we wouldn't pray or have religion anymore. Instead, we sang "Deutschland, Deutschland, Uber Alles," and had physical education. Sunday became National Youth Day with compulsory attendance. Parents were not pleased about the sudden change in curriculum. They were told that if they did not send us, they would receive a stiff letter of warning the first time. The second time they would be fined the equivalent of $300, and the third time they would be subject to jail. The first two hours consisted of political indoctrination. The rest of the day we had sports. As time went along, we loved it. Oh, we had so much fun and got our sports equipment free. We would go home and gleefully tell our parents about the wonderful time we had.

My mother was very unhappy. When the next term started, she took me out of public school and put me in a convent. I told her she couldn't do that and she told me that someday when I grew up, I would be grateful. There was a very good curriculum, but hardly any fun - no sports, and no political indoctrination. I hated it at first but felt I could tolerate it. Every once in a while, on holidays, I went home. I would go back to my old friends and ask what was going on and what they were doing. Their loose lifestyle was very alarming to me. They lived without religion. By that time unwed mothers were glorified for having a baby for Hitler. It seemed strange to me that our society changed so suddenly. As time went along, I realized what a great deed my mother did so that I wasn't exposed to that kind of humanistic philosophy.

EQUAL RIGHTS HITS HOME

In 1939, the war started and a food bank was established. All food was rationed and could only be purchased using food stamps. At the same time, a full-employment law was passed which meant if you didn't work, you didn't get a ration card, and if you didn't have a card, you starved to death. Women who stayed home to raise their families didn't have any marketable skills and often had to take jobs more suited for men. Soon after this, the draft was implemented. It was compulsory for young people, male and female, to give one year to the labor corps. During the day, the girls worked on the farms, and at night they returned to their barracks for military training just like the boys. They were trained to be anti-aircraft gunners and participated in the signal corps. After the labor corps, they were not discharged but were used in the front lines. When I go back to Austria to visit my family and friends, most of these women are emotional cripples because they just were not equipped to handle the horrors of combat. Three months before I turned 18, I was severely injured in an air raid attack. I nearly had a leg amputated, so I was spared having to go into the labor corps and into military service.

Hitler Restructured the Family Through Daycare: When the mothers had to go out into the work force, the government immediately established child care centers. You could take your children ages 4 weeks to school age and leave them there around-the-clock, 7 days a week, under the total care of the government. The state raised a whole generation of children. There were no motherly women to take care of the children, just people highly trained in child psychology. By this time, no one talked about equal rights. We knew we had been had."

HEALTH CARE AND SMALL BUSINESS SUFFER UNDER GOVERNMENT CONTROLS:

Before Hitler, we had very good medical care. Many American doctors trained at the University of Vienna. After Hitler, health care was socialized, free for everyone. Doctors were salaried by the government. The problem was, since it was free, the people were going to the doctors for everything. When the good doctor arrived at his office at 8 a.m., 40 people were already waiting and, at the same time, the hospitals were full. If you needed elective surgery, you had to wait a year or two for your turn. There was no money for research as it was poured into socialized medicine. Research at the medical schools literally stopped, so the best doctors left Austria and emigrated to other countries.

As for healthcare, our tax rates went up to 80% of our income. Newlyweds immediately received a $1,000 loan from the government to establish a household. We had big programs for families. All day care and education were free. High schools were taken over by the government and college tuition was subsidized. Everyone was entitled to free handouts, such as food stamps, clothing, and housing.

We had another agency designed to monitor business. My brother-in-law owned a restaurant that had square tables. Government officials told him he had to replace them with round tables because people might bump themselves on the corners. Then they said he had to have additional bathroom facilities. It was just a small dairy business with a snack bar. He couldn't meet all the demands. Soon, he went out of business. If the government owned the large businesses and not many small ones existed, it could be in control.

We had consumer protection. We were told how to shop and what to buy. Free enterprise was essentially abolished. We had a planning agency specially designed for farmers. The agents would go to the farms, count the live-stock, then tell the farmers what to produce, and how to produce it.

"MERCY KILLING" REDEFINED:

In 1944, I was a student teacher in a small village in the Alps. The villagers were surrounded by mountain passes which, in the winter, were closed off with snow, causing people to be isolated. So people intermarried and offspring were sometimes retarded.

When I arrived, I was told there were 15 mentally retarded adults, but they were all useful and did good manual work. I knew one, named Vincent, very well. He was a janitor of the school. One day I looked out the window and saw Vincent and others getting into a van. I asked my superior where they were going. She said to an institution where the State Health Department would teach them a trade, and to read and write. The families were required to sign papers with a little clause that they could not visit for 6 months. They were told visits would interfere with the program and might cause homesickness.

As time passed, letters started to dribble back saying these people died a natural, merciful death. The villagers were not fooled. We suspected what was happening. Those people left in excellent physical health and all died within 6 months. We called this euthanasia.

THE FINAL STEPS - GUN LAWS:

Next came gun registration. People were getting injured by guns. Hitler said that the real way to catch criminals (we still had a few) was by matching serial numbers on guns. Most citizens were law abiding and dutifully marched to the police station to register their firearms. Not long after-wards, the police said that it was best for everyone to turn in their guns. The authorities already knew who had them, so it was futile not to comply voluntarily.

No more freedom of speech. Anyone who said something against the government was taken away. We knew many people who were arrested, not only Jews, but also priests and ministers who spoke up.

Totalitarianism didn't come quickly, it took 5 years from 1938 until 1943, to realize full dictatorship in Austria. Had it happened overnight, my countrymen would have fought to the last breath. Instead, we had creeping gradualism. Now, our only weapons were broom handles. The whole idea sounds almost unbelievable that the state, little by little eroded our freedom. After World War II, Russian troops occupied Austria . Women were raped, preteen to elderly. The press never wrote about this either. When the Soviets left in 1955, they took everything that they could, dismantling whole factories in the process. They sawed down whole orchards of fruit, and what they couldn't destroy, they burned. We called it The Burned Earth. Most of the population barricaded themselves in their houses. Women hid in their cellars for 6 weeks as the troops mobilized. Those who couldn't, paid the price. There is a monument in Vienna today, dedicated to those women who were massacred by the Russians.

This is an eye witness account."

"It's true...those of us who sailed past the Statue of Liberty came to a country of unbelievable freedom and opportunity.

America Truly is the Greatest Country in the World. Don't Let Freedom Slip Away.

After America , There is No Place to Go"

(Source retrieved on 7-15-10 at http://www.aipnews.com/talk/forums/thread-view.asp?tid=12514&posts=7)

THE FEDERAL RESERVE- ENEMY OF AMERICA

The "Federal Reserve-Enemy of America" by G. Edward Griffen is an exemplary tale of the nefarious private international bank that has financially enslaved Americans. Mr. Griffen reports the alleged "Feds" have managed to conceal from most of the American public their criminal scheme to deprive Americans of their wealth. It is a book that will open your eyes to these evil money-mongers who are stealing our citizens' ability to financially survive.

The Federal Reserve is a fraud. It is a private bank of international bankers that have taken over our government. It is a money scam that puts the Ponzi scheme and the Social Security racquet to shame. Social Security, incidentally, is a racquet as well. More than 56 trillion dollars has been taken out of the so-called Social Security lock box and replaced with lOU's. A "legal theft" has occurred and no one is going to prison. The word, "racquet" is as valid as Al Capone's Chicago activities.

Mr. Griffen points out that Thomas D. Schauf, CPA, has expended a great deal of time describing the fraud perpetrated by the Federal Reserve in his book entitled "The Federal Reserve History." In "The Federal Reserve History" he gives the background on the private corporation that most Americans, erroneously, still think is part of the federal government. For the disbelievers it would be prudent to read the Federal Reserve Act of 1913. It can be googled.

Mr. Griffen, once again, refers to another source-Sheldon Emery. Mr. Emery has summarized the essence of this fraud in the classic "Billions for the Bankers, Debt for the People". He states *"But even after all this evidence, the public still refuses to face the trepidation-that they are living within a controlled economic system that is ruled by elites, while the masses pay all the bills."*— Sheldon Emery.

And yet, another warning. The treachery against the nation is seen in the final inference by William Greider in his book "Secrets of the Temple." This author concludes *"If people crave comfort in denial and solace in the company of weak-willed citizens, America is surely doomed. There can be no intelligent debate about the merits of the Federal Reserve. It is pure Fraud. Fractional reserve banking is criminal. Public indebtedness, as a requirement for currency creation is the supreme Treason."*

For the uninitiated, fractional banking is a form of counterfeiting that the banking system has been getting away with for over two hundred years. Should a citizen deposit $1,000 dollars into his account, the bankers multiply that sum by nine times and print currency, in this case, equal to nine thousand more dollars. The nine thousand dollars are then loaned out with interest in spite of the fact there is no rationale for printing that "extra" money. It is not backed up by anything of value and is pure unadulterated fraud. This form of counterfeiting would place private individuals in prison serving hard-time. It must be rectified in our lifetime.

Sheldon Emery continues with a condemnation of U.S. citizens: "So *why does the American public continue to wear the chains of serfdom so willingly? The answer is obvious. The citizens of this great land don't deserve to be called Americans! They have become hollow tools of the insidious propaganda that tells them that your own property is really not yours. They have accepted their status as slaves to a money racquet that destroys their lives and relegates them to a hopeless future. But their greatest sin is that they embrace the mythology in this satanic region of an unconstitutional money monopoly."*

In my personal view, Presidents of the United States had to be aware of the insidious and evil money-mongers that have financially raped the American taxpayer. We can only guess that these so-called national leaders were complicit, cowards or simply ignorant. In all three categories—none of them—deserved to be Presidents of the United States. The conclusion must be that no one should seek the office of the presidency unless he or she has the courage and the skill to repeal the Federal Reserve act of 1913 and re-institute the U. S. Treasury as the sole agency for our financial destiny. The Founders would be been proud to have Article 1, Section 8 of the Constitution restored. The presidents who resisted the central banks and were assaulted or assassinated deserve our utmost respect.

The author of the article, the "Federal Reserve-Enemy of America", quotes an outspoken congressional enemy of the Federal Reserve—Congressman McFadden. Congressman Louis T. McFadden on May 23 of 1933 brought impeachment charges against the members of the Federal Reserve:

"Whereas I charge them jointly and severally with having brought about a repudiation of the national currency of the United States in order that gold value of said currency might be given to private interests.

I charge them with having arbitrarily and unlawfully taken over $80,000,000,000 from the United States government in the year 1928

I charge them...with having brought about the decline of prices on the New York Stock Exchange...

I charge them. ..with having conspired to transfer to foreigners and international money lenders, title to control of the financial resources of the United States...

I charge them...with having published false and misleading propaganda intended to deceive the American people and to cause the United States to lose its independence.

I charge them...with the crime of having treasonably conspired and acted against the peace and security of the United State, and with having treasonably conspired to destroy the constitutional government of the United States."—The aforementioned quote was published by G. Edward Griffen and is available in the Congressional Records.

An American hero—Congressman McFadden was assaulted three times by gunfire and twice by poisoning. The Congressman expired after the second poisoning in 1936.

Supplemental explanations were written and quotes selected by Sal Terrusa

Source: G. Edward GRIFFEN Google the" "Federal Reserve-Enemy of America" for the entire article-an excellent explanation of the Federal Reserve's role in the financial exploitation of Americans.

PATRIOTS OF THE REVOLUTION
Reprinted with permission

* Words we'd best remember...

"You will never know how much it cost us to preserve your freedom. I hope that you will make a good use of it. If you do not, I shall repent in heaven that I ever took half the pains to preserve it."

—John Adams

Pastor Rob quotes Thomas Paine, tells of George Washington:
"Last Sunday it seemed as if Pastor Rob, at times, spoke just for us! He encouraged people to get active to preserve their freedom. He quoted the Declaration of Independence - "life, liberty & the pursuit of happiness" He told how, on Christmas Day 1776, George Washington gave to each of his troops — dwindled down from 30,000 to a mere 2,500, a third without boots, their feet wrapped in burlap and leaving bloody footprints in the snow — Thomas Paines' words before they crossed the Delaware:

"These are the times that try men's souls. The summer soldier and the sunshine patriot will, in this crisis, shrink from the service of their country; but he that stands by it now, deserves the love and thanks of man and woman. Tyranny, like hell, is not easily conquered, yet we have this consolation with us, that the harder the conflict, the more glorious the triumph. What we obtain too cheap, we esteem too lightly: it is dearness only that gives every

thing its value. Heaven knows how to put a proper price upon its goods; and it would be strange indeed if so celestial an article as FREEDOM should not be highly rated. ..."

—*Thomas Paine*

And so we began with words of John Adams and end with words of Thomas Paine and valor of George Washington, and encouragement from Pastor Rob for more people to become active in preserving the FREEDOM the Founding Founders gave us!"

A Special Expression of Gratitude:

Thank you Carolyn Guillet for making more Tea Partiers aware of George Washington's timely use of Thomas Paine's immortal words. Your efforts and leadership in the Tea Party movement are very much appreciated.

—Sal Terrusa

THE 545 PEOPLE
By Charlie Reese

All Americans should be exposed to the truth about us and the Congress of the United States as Charlie Reese saw it. A few quotes to sample Charlie's wisdom and then a website so that you can enjoy the rest of the story. Charlie has other versions and articles which have been updated from time to time. I thought you might find the following article from snopes.com interesting: The following article was first written in 1985 and published in 1995. Enjoy the excerpts!

"Politicians are the only people in the world that creates problems and then campaign against them. Have you ever wondered if both the Democrats and the Republicans are against deficits, WHY do we have deficits? You and I don't propose a federal budget. The president does. You and I don't write the tax code, Congress does. You and I don't set fiscal policy, Congress does. You and I don't control monetary policy, the Federal Reserve Bank does. One hundred senators, 435 congressmen, one president, and nine Supreme Court justices equates to 545 human beings out of the 310 million are directly, legally, morally, and individually responsible for the domestic problems that plague this country. I excluded the members of the Federal Reserve Board because that problem was created by the Congress. In 1913, Congress delegated its Constitutional duty to provide a sound currency to a federally chartered, but private, central bank. I excluded all the special interests and lobbyists for a sound reason. They have no ability to coerce a senator, a congressman, or a president to do one cotton-

picking thing."

It is extremely perceptive of Mr. Reese to place the irresponsibility of congress as the root of all our governmental problems. I love Charlie Reese and wouldn't change a word of what he has said. Charlie has inspired some thoughts, however, that should be emphasized. The Federal Reserve, in my opinion, is the primary cause of the nation's inability to maintain economic stability. There is another element to congressional failures. The voters are too slow to react and remove the incompetents from public office. Note the source below for more of Charlie Reese. Let's have a few more quotes.

"I don't care if they offer a politician $1 million dollars in cash. The politician has the power to accept or reject it. No matter what the lobbyist promises, it is the legislator's responsibility to determine how he votes. Those 545 human beings spend much of their energy convincing you that what they did is not their fault. They cooperate in this common con regardless of party. The president can only propose a budget. He cannot force the Congress to accept it. Who is the speaker of the House? Nancy Pelosi. She is the leader of the majority party. She and fellow House members, not the president, can approve any budget they want. If the president vetoes it, they can pass it over his veto... It seems inconceivable to me that a nation of 310 million cannot replace 545 people who stand convicted - by present facts — of incompetence and irresponsibility. If the tax code is unfair, it's because they want it unfair. If the budget is in the red, it's because they want it in the red. If they do not receive social security but are on an elite retirement plan not available to the people, it's because they want it that way. There are no insoluble government problems. Do not let these 545 people shift the blame to bureaucrats, whom they hire. We should vote all of them out of office and clean up their mess!"

Honesty in government has gone by the wayside and corruption is rampant We may need one more volunteer group made up of citizens—they shall be known as the "truth" police. You can find the rest of the story and articles by contacting the source below. Thank you Charlie for reminding us about who is responsible and saying it the way it is.

http://www.snopes.com/politics/soapbox/reese.asp

From an Obama classmate:
WAYNE ALLYN ROOT: OVERWHELM THE SYSTEM
Reprinted by Permission

"Barrack Obama is no fool. He is not incompetent. To the contrary, he is brilliant. He knows exactly what he's doing. He is purposely overwhelming the U.S. economy to create systemic failure, economic crisis and social chaos — thereby destroying capitalism and our country from within.

Barack Obama is my college classmate (Columbia University, class of '83). As Glenn Beck correctly predicted from day one, Obama is following the plan of Cloward & Piven, two professors at Columbia University. They outlined a plan to socialize America by overwhelming the system with government spending and entitlement demands. Add up the clues below. Taken individually they're alarming. Taken as a whole, it is a brilliant, Machiavellian game plan to turn the United States into a socialist/Marxist state with a permanent majority that desperately needs government for survival... and can be counted on to always vote for bigger government. Why not? They have no responsibility to pay for it.

• Universal health care. The health care bill had very little to do with health care. It had everything to do with unionizing millions of hospital and health care workers, as well as adding 15,000 to 20,000 new IRS agents (who will join government employee unions).Obama doesn't care that giving free health care to

30 million Americans will add trillions to the national debt. What he does care about is that it cements the dependence of those 30 million voters to Democrats and big government. Who but a socialist revolutionary would pass this reckless spending bill in the middle of a depression?

• Cap and trade. Like health care legislation having nothing to do with health care, cap and trade has nothing to do with global warming. It has everything to do with redistribution of income, government control of the economy and a criminal payoff to Obama's biggest contributors. Those powerful and wealthy unions and contributors (like GE, which owns NBC, MSNBC and CNBC) can then be counted on to support everything Obama wants. They will kickback hundreds of millions of dollars in contributions to Obama and the Democratic Party to keep them in power. The bonus is that all the new taxes on Americans with bigger cars, bigger homes and businesses helps Obama 'spread the wealth around.'

• Make Puerto Rico a state. Why? Who's asking for a 51st state? Who's asking for millions of new welfare recipients and government entitlement addicts in the middle of a depression? Certainly not American taxpayers. But this has been Obama's plan all along. His goal is to add two new Democrat senators, five Democrat congressman and a million loyal Democratic voters who are dependent on big government.

• Legalize 12 million illegal immigrants. Just giving these 12 million potential new citizens free health care alone could overwhelm the system and bankrupt America. But it adds 12 million reliable new Democrat voters who can be counted on to support big government. Add another few trillion dollars in welfare, aid to dependent children, food stamps, free medical, education, tax credits for the poor, and eventually Social Security.

• Stimulus and bailouts. Where did all that money go? It went to Democrat contributors, organizations (ACORN), and unions - including billions of dollars to save or create jobs of government employees across the country. It went to save GM and Chrysler so that their employees could keep paying union dues. It went to AIG so that Goldman Sachs could be bailed out (after giving Obama almost $1 million in contributions). A staggering $125 billion went to teachers (thereby protecting their union dues). All those public employees will vote loyally Democrat to protect their bloated salaries and pensions that are bankrupting America. The country goes broke, future generations face a bleak future, but Obama, the Democrat Party, government, and the unions grow more powerful. The ends justify the means.

Raise taxes on small business owners, high-income earners, and job creators. Put the entire burden on only the top 20 ercent of taxpayers, redistribute the income, punish success, and reward those who did nothing to deserve it (except vote for Obama). Reagan wanted to dramatically cut taxes in order to starve the government. Obama wants to dramatically raise taxes to starve his political opposition.

With the acts outlined above, Obama and his regime have created a vast and rapidly expanding constituency of voters dependent on big government; a vast privileged class of public employees who work for big government; and a government dedicated to destroying capitalism and installing themselves as socialist rulers by overwhelming the system.

Add it up and you've got the perfect Marxist scheme - all devised by my Columbia University college classmate Barack Obama using the Cloward and Piven Plan."

Thank You Wayne Allyn Root for sharing your experience with Barak Hussein Obama when he was a classmate of yours.

—S. Terrusa

FINANCIAL REFORM OR BUST
Reprinted by Permission

The American heritage of freedom and economic opportunity has been eroding for the past century. Corporations and companies paid an Ad Valorum Tax (a property tax) as the main source of federal revenue in 1912.

The usual duties, imposts, excise taxes and tariffs were in play, as well. It was against constitutional law to directly tax the individual (a capitation tax).

Our economy was booming in comparison to other competing nations. President Teddy Roosevelt paraded a fleet of warships around the world to let the major powers know the U.S. had arrived and was ready to play with the big boys.

We must regain our lost heritage of freedoms and equal economic opportunity by abolishing the "phony" Federal Reserve and replacing the income tax with the pre-1913 Ad Valorum tax system.

The individual would not pay a direct tax.

An alternative Business Tax: A fixed tax limit based on a percentage of the Gross Domestic Product (GDP) would be established for corporations and companies. The percentage would be large enough to sustain the federal government after it has been reduced by 50% of its well-known waste. Mr. Glenn Beck's research team has performed the same function of President Reagan's Grace Commission—the extravagant waste discovered may exceed 50% of the current federal budget.

A Business Tax based on 10% of the Gross Domestic Product for corporations and companies (omitting the tax on individuals) would result in 1.46 trillion dollars of federal revenue. The Gross Domestic Product (GDP) for 2010 is projected to be more than 14,600 billions of dollars. Take home pay would increase by 40% to 45%. The individual would be able to pay for his or her own health and retirement plans. Understanding simple arithmetic makes the plan doable unless you're not smarter than a 5th grader. Taxes would be much lower and tax revenues would be more than adequate.

The initiative of the Income Tax Amendment in 1913, during the winter recess of congress, permitted a few conspiratorial Senators to push the new law forward without the usual debate. The Income Tax allowed congress to tax individuals virtually without restraint. Everything one earns or owns could be taken from you by over-taxation. The constitution of our Founders prohibited such a potentionally economic catastrophic event to take place. Corrupt bankers and politicians overturned a federal tax system that allowed individual Americans to maintain a constitutional right to keep the greater fruits of one's labors. The states, however, had and still have the option to tax or not tax its citizens.

In 2010, between 50% and 60% of most American wages or salaries have been taxed from multiple sources. Included in the entire taxation of citizens are federal, state, and local consumer taxes. Let us not forget the taxes on alcohol, tobacco, gasoline, utilities, recycling and other hidden taxes too numerous to mention.

Another great obstacle to economic stability occurred in 1913, as well. The Federal Reserve Act replaced the constitutional functions of the U.S. Treasury. The fallaciously entitled "Federal Reserve" is a private corporation of international bankers whose primary fiduciary duty is to mostly foreign shareholders. The so-called "Feds" used their profits for themselves as well and did not and have not paid taxes to the U.S. government. The American taxpayer is a customer and not the owners of the central bank known as the Federal Reserve.

The international cartel known as the Federal Reserve has been creating economic chaos whenever it served its interest. The Great Depression of 1929, and the most recent on-going recession among several others in our history, can be traced to the purposeful designs of this self-serving group—at the expense of the American taxpayer.

Americans must heed the wisdom of our founders and re-institute the U.S. Treasury to print our own currency and set the interest rates. Profits from U.S. loans to borrowers would serve the interest of American citizens, not the Federal Reserve and its shareholders.

We must regain our lost heritage of freedoms and equal economic opportunity by abolishing the "phony" Federal Reserve and replacing the income tax with the pre-1913 Ad Valorum Tax system or a Business Tax. The individual would not pay a direct tax. A fixed tax limit based a on a percentage of the Gross Domestic Product (GDP) would be established for corporations and companies. The percentage would be large enough to sustain the federal government after it has been reduced by 50% of its well-known waste. Mr. Beck's research team has performed the function of President Reagan's Grace Commission—the extravagant waste may exceed 50% of the current federal budget.

The federal government has economically failed and is more than 14 trillion dollars in debt. The states should take-over Medicare and Social Security along with the funding until the private sector eventually replaces the states' involvement. The states are in close proximity to offer services and monitor the revenues with far more efficiency and fairness.

All other reforms presented in the book entitled "Patriot Papers" would be more easily accomplished after successfully resolving two major issues:

1. Abolishing the 16th Amendment known as the Income Tax Amendment.

2. Abolishing the Federal Reserve Act.

The other reforms in the book must be pursued for a more secure and prosperous nation.

Long live our proven patriots and damn the foreign and national parasites.

—Jo Terrusa

PART 4

INTRODUCTION to Part 4

Conclusions and Solutions

American *exceptionalism* has created a nation second to none in terms of prosperity and security. The perpetuation of its uniqueness relies on the knowledge of American history and the proper pursuit of economic stability. A rapid recovery from the Great Recession is offered through an understanding of the following salient points and taking the necessary actions:

POWER
　The uniqueness of self-rule and its role has contributed to the successful American political experiment.

THE GENERAL WELFARE CLAUSE
　How the judiciary has vastly distorted the intent of the constitution.

A SIMPLISTIC REMEDY FOR DISTORTIONS OF
THE CONSTITUTION
　The U.S. Constitution does not need to be *interpreted* before deciding on an issue before the courts.

A QUICK FIX FOR THE CURRENT ECONOMY

Return $160 billion dollars to the states; a sum hoarded by the "unconstitutional" Federal Department of Education (D.O.E.)

THE REAL OWNERS OF THE FEDERAL RESERVE

It is necessary to reinstitute the U.S. Treasury while repealing the Federal Reserve Act of 1913. A majority of *foreigners* have wreaked economic havoc with our economy for more than 90 years. The fallacious Federal Reserve must go—these increasingly greedy international bankers must be banned from our shores.

HOW TO JOIN A TEA PARTY

Your voice will be heard loud and clear by joining a local Tea Party. Become a member of an unstoppable patriotic force to recapture governmental sanity for yourself and your family's posterity.

FUTURE CANDIDATES FOR PUBLIC OFFICE

Should you run for public office and require Tea Party support—complete and sign the pledge to *present, promote and vote* for the relevant issues of our times.

CONSTITUTIONAL ENACTMENTS

The urgent resolve of these three highest priorities will provide a more rapid march to an increase in the nation's exceptionalism.

THE REST OF THE STORY

The remaining significant issues must be confronted and resolved to consummate America's greatness. The love of freedom has been purchased with the blood of millions of our fellow Americans.

We, the living, have a duty to honor their sacrifice.

POWER

The People of the United States possess the power and title as the ultimate rulers for each level of government: Local, State and Federal.

The people use that power to select candidates for public office by their vote—the most successful candidates become public officials.

The people lend that power to newly elected officials to represent their views and to perform the *honorable* execution of duty.

The people may use their power and discretion to recall, impeach or remove a public official for malfeasance immediately or at the next election.

The American political experiment has replaced absolute rulers, kings, emperors, dictators and tyrants with elected public officials and controlled limits to their time of service.

The historical concept of a Republic is relatively new—only 223 years has passed since the U.S. Constitution was instituted in 1787. How successful has it been? The Gross Domestic Product of the United States is **14.1 times greater** than its closest economic rival— which happens to be China.

The problem of venal politicians, however, is still problematic and a grave threat to the Republic.

"May the ultimate powers of the American people meet each and every challenge to cherished American freedoms"
—Sal Terrusa

THE GENERAL WELFARE CLAUSE

The General Welfare clause of the constitution as created by Dr. Samuel Johnson was defined in those days as the "happiness, success and prosperity of the people" according to his English-language dictionary which was prevalent in the 1780s.

The people within the states were responsible for the General Welfare, not the federal government. The Founders also believed in those days that competition among the states would enhance the General Welfare. The Founders definitely believed the responsibility for the needy were relatives, friends, neighbors, church and community; and, possibly, the individual states but never the federal government.

Modern politicians expanded the General Welfare clause beyond its original meaning.

Large unaffordable federal governmental programs such as Social Security, Medicare, healthcare, prescriptions for the elderly, earmarks, and welfare for the poor, loans to foreign countries, construction for roads and bridges with multiple duplicative bureaucracies, etc., etc. were never meant to be federal programs.

Our Founders further understood an over-sized federal government would lead to uncontrollable waste, less prosperity and a weakened military. The current generation of politicians has proved the Founders correct—we are presently more than 14 trillion dollars in debt and approaching national bankruptcy.

Lower taxes would permit citizens to pay for their own retirement and medical needs. The quality and cost of service in the private sector improves with competition. Competition is absent in a single monopolistic government plan.

Politicians would promise us the moon to be re-elected; their kept promises are costing us trillions of dollars. Earmarks have contributed to our indebtedness. The" Big Dig "in Boston originally was for three billion dollars. It has reached the fifteen billion mark and is still climbing. Those Earmark sums happen to come from Americans who don't live in Boston. "How fair is that" said Peter while paying Paul? Robbing Peter to pay Paul is "theft" within or without the government. Venal career politicians are responsible for the current financial mess. Congress has achieved the lowest rating in American history with an eleven percent approval rating.

Earmarks should be banished in favor of long term and low interest rate loans for congressional districts that truly need funds for honest projects. Let's stop draining the U.S. Treasury. Politicians use the *free money*, called Earmarks, to purchase votes for re-election. How fair is that in the competition for elected public office?

National defense, international affairs and Interstate commerce may be the only functions of the Federal government. Have you ever wondered why the feds are duplicating bureaucracies that already exist in the states? Billions are being wasted.

Unnecessary spending is the outright theft of our labors.

Join your fellow patriots in keeping each and every politician's feet to the fire regardless of political affiliation. Citizens must be the deciders of tax limitations via a call for a new referendum—Congress has failed us big time. A referendum by the people would control how much *we say* congress can spend.

Citizen commissions are needed to monitor all levels of government.

The Commissioners could be selected from a jury type pool and remain incognito to avoid contact with corrupt politicians and lobbyists with deep pockets and promises.

No country's government should be large enough to fail.

It is far better to spread the risk over fifty independent and sovereign American states. The States and its people created the federal government and they have the power to re-direct that government. The states and its people have done it thus far with 27 amendments.

"The greedy global bankers and industrial elitists must fail in their goal for a One World Government. A two- tier society: Those who rule and those who serve the rulers must also fail."

—Sal Terrusa

A SIMPLISTIC REMEDY
FOR DISTORTIONS OF THE CONSTITUTION

The U.S. Constitution does not need to be *interpreted* before deciding on an issue before the courts.

The primary consideration: Does the issue fall within the province of the federal Government. If so, rule on the issue. There is no need to *interpret* the meaning. The Constitution is not unlike a contract between or among individuals. The wording of the contract or document has been accepted by all parties and endorsed or certified by their signatures. A court of jurisdiction simply has to read the agreed upon contract or document and make a ruling. If the contract or document is unclear then it becomes null and void. If an issue within the constitution becomes unclear or outdated the remedy is to amend it with an acceptable version— an example, the repeal of prohibition (the 21st Amendment).

Interpreting the constitution is a form of lawmaking from the bench; a procedure that may be inaccurate and, at best, unwise. The nine justices on the Supreme Court may have nine different versions or *interpretations* of an issue. *Interpretation* is a form of guesswork.

Rule or amend. It's that simple.

A QUICK FIX FOR THE CURRENT ECONOMY

The Federal Department of Education ignored the 10th Amendment which prohibits issues not scripted in the U.S. Constitution as a right belonging to the states or to the people. The unscripted Federal Department of Education, consequently, is unconstitutional by that definition.

The Founders did not want a central government to become all powerful. The control of education by a federal government would place the government in position to propagandize or brainwash the nation's children. Controlling the minds of the nation's children could lead to eventual tyranny and/or limited educational opportunities in the absence of competition among the states.

Originally, the nation's independent states did not want a central government compromising their sovereignty. The states believed competition among the states for educational excellence and sharing the successes would benefit all the states; a result far more desirable than the current one-size-fits-all program.

The Department of Education had its budget increased from a little more than 82 billion in 2009 to more than 160 billion in 2010. Returning more than $160 billion dollars, presently being hoarded by the Federal Department of Education, to the states would allow every state including California, for example, to have had a balanced budget in 2010.

California represents at least 12% of the 310 million people living in the United States. California would receive almost $20 billion dollars instead of the less than the $3.5 billion dollars received from the stimulus fund (also paid for by American taxpayer). If California would be out of debt by this action, the other 49 states may be in surplus. Thus, a quick fix.

The Federal Department of Education (D.O.E) would expect the states, of course, to assume the mandated as well as the discretionary funding. The funds currently budgeted for the D.O.E. should be immediately returned to *all the states* during these difficult economic times.

A QUICK FIX, as suggested above, would instantly relieve the states and its residents who are suffering during these difficult times. It would provide instant relief until more permanent solutions could be found.

THE REAL OWNERS OF THE FEDERAL RESERVE BANKS:

Note: Reprinted for non-believers and readers who may have overlooked the significance of foreigners dictating our economic destiny for their self-interests.

Rothschild Bank of *London*
Rothschild Bank of *Berlin*
Lazard Brothers of *Paris*
Israel Moses Seif Banks of *Italy*
Warburg Bank of *Amsterdam*
Warburg Bank of *Hamburg*
Lehman Brothers of New York*
Kuhn Loeb Bank of New York
Goldman, Sachs of New York
Chase Manhattan Bank of New York

*Lehman Brothers of N.Y. has failed and is no longer in business.

The Federal Reserve is a private corporation of international bankers. The bank operates for profit and has a fiduciary duty to its shareholders. The bank owners and their shareholders, as you have witnessed above, are predominantly foreigners. The so-called "Feds" primary responsibility is not to the American taxpayer but to their shareholders.

American taxpayers, in fact, have been bailing out the failing banks who are the customers of the Federal Reserve. The U.S government foolishly accepts loans from the Federal Reserve for the bailouts and must not only pay interest on those loans but put up enormous bonuses or fees as security for the loans.

Why didn't the Feds bailout their own string of customers?

American taxpayers were suckered into more indebtedness because we have corrupt high officials cooperating with these international money-mongers. These phony "Feds" contribute campaign funds to both sides of the aisle.

The United States Treasury has had its constitutional duty usurped and is not able to earn interest on loans due the nation's indebtedness— thanks to the Federal Reserve and their venal co-conspirators.

The Federal Reserve does not pay American taxes due to their foreign status.

We have not been able to audit the "Feds" but they have former employees from their bank in high positions of the U.S. Government. Secretary of the Treasury, Tim Geithner, was a former bank president of the New York Federal Reserve. Spies in high places!? We don't know what they are doing— but Secretary Geithner has full access to our financial affairs.

We need American patriots in charge of our financial affairs–not self-serving former employees of a foreign bank.

HOW TO JOIN A TEA PARTY

Tea Party members and other fellow Americans believe in responsible fiscal policy, constitutional limitations and fair opportunities within a free-market economy.

If you choose to join your fellow patriots, contact a local Tea Party by an Internet search using the words "Tea Party" and your city. Example: Search for Tea Party Santa Barbara.

The vast majority of Americans believe in candidates for public office taking action on the issues represented on the following page. Before the next election cycle, please feel free to make a copy or copies of these "Constitutional Enactments/Statues".

Send a copy or copies to your local candidates running for public office and learn of their responses. If they fail to return a signed copy, it is time to consider another candidate.

An exception: A candidate commenting on a way that would move us more closely to a more equitable political system. Americans appreciate superior ways to advance the American experiment. If you have an idea that *is* being overlooked—speak up!

You may choose to run for public office, as well.

FUTURE CANDIDATES FOR PUBLIC OFFICE

Candidates for public office who believe in taking personal action on the issues represented on the following page i.e., "Constitutional Enactments/Statues" should make a copy of the pledge on page 225, complete the information required, sign at the bottom of the page and submit it to your local Tea Party organization. It would be prudent to declare your candidacy before the next election cycle, sooner rather than later, in preparing a possible run for public office. Send your signed pledge to your local Tea Party organization.

Your vote as a citizen or as a candidate will redirect the political course we must take to retain America's greatness.

CONSTITUTIONAL ENACTMENTS AND STATUTES

Repeal the Federal Reserve Act of 1913. These international banksters serve mostly foreign shareholders–not the American taxpayer. Global money-mongers, fallaciously known as the "Federal Reserve", must be eliminated. Let's, once again, print our own money and stop the borrowing. Corrupt foreigners such as the deceptively named "Feds""destroy our economy via fractional-banking (a euphemism for fraud and counterfeiting).

The Federal Reserve has usurped the power which, at one time, belonged to the U.S. Treasury. The Federal Reserve has been foisting undesirable loans on the American taxpayer whether we, the taxpayers, like it or not. We are forced to pay the interest on these unwanted loans. A bonus, in addition to the interest charged is assessed to larger loans, further increasing the interest and debt.

We must abolish these international financial parasites and re-institute the U.S. Treasury. Re-establishment of the duties of the U.S. Treasury under Article 1 Section 8 of the original constitution would return sanity to our national finances.

A balanced budget Amendment would eliminate the need for money from the so-called "Feds". Cutting spending, not borrowing would be the proper course of action. Pass a balanced budget amendment by 2012 or sooner, if possible. Congress has failed miserably in protecting the U.S. treasury.

Replace the Federal Income Tax with the Ad Valorum Tax of 1912 (a property tax) – only corporations and companies paid these taxes – individuals did not pay any taxes. Remove thousands of IRS agents from the payroll. U.S. treasury agents would be able to handle the vastly reduced number of collections.

An alternative tax code would be to assess 6% of the gross domestic product (GDP) on corporations and businesses only. The individual, again, would not be subject to a direct tax. Such a tax in 2010 would have provided $840 Billion dollars– this is more than double what the government should be spending. Glenn Beck's researchers concluded 50 % of government is **waste.**

Enact a referendum (a vote by citizens) to establish tax limits or increases in the tax code for any reason, including war. We cannot afford to refer this vital issue exclusively to our representatives in congress.

The president has been limited to two four year terms by the 22nd amendment. The presidency is the only public office that justifies more than one term due to the rare and critical global power of the position.

Enact a single term limit of four years for the House of Representatives and six years for the Senate. We must limit the power, influence and corruption associated with career or multiple-term politicians.

IN THE INTERIM:

We should have lowered all taxes below the Bush Tax Cuts prior to December 31, 2010 until permanent legislation and a new tax code is enacted. Lowering all taxes at this time is necessary to stabilize the economy and eliminate the need for international money- monger's loans.

It is still not too late to abolish all the following unfair and unnecessary federal taxes immediately to spur the economy: Marriage tax, Death Tax, Alternative Minimum tax, Capital Gains Tax, Social Security taxes, Taxes on dividends, Taxes on gas, alcohol, tobacco, and computer recycling, etc. Let's make the U.S. more competitive in the global economy as rapidly as possible.

The states and its people are responsible for the Common Welfare and entitlements—not the federal government. Read pages 66 and 67 for clarification.

The author prefers a new tax for corporations and companies ONLY based on 6% of the GDP. Individuals would not be directly taxed. Take-home pay would increase by more than 40 %. If you have a better taxation plan—share it. Let's not keep it a secret.

Successful Tea Party incumbents must initiate legislation to achieve the aforementioned goals. Incumbents refusing to support these issues must be replaced at the next elections in 2012.

CANDIDATES FOR PUBLIC OFFICE PLEDGE

WARNING!!!

Attention: Candidates for Public Office – Failure to pledge to work toward the following **basic issues** may negatively impact Tea Party support:

REPEAL THE FEDERAL RESERVE ACT 1913. We must dump the number one trouble-maker of our national debt. The Feds are a private corporation of international bankers and foreign shareholders–not a US. Bank.

REPEAL THE INCOME TAX. Over-taxation without limits leads to economic slavery. Replace with a Business tax based on the GDP for corporations and companies ONLY. No taxes on the individual. Restore high employment. Revenues would equal $840 billion dollars @ 6% of the 2009 GDP – twice what we need after cutting government waste.

ENACT A TERM LIMIT. Enact a single term limit of four years for the House of Representatives and six years for the Senate.

To be filled in by candidate:

Your signature below acknowledges a pledge on your honor to present, promote and vote for all of the above if elected.

Signature_____
Name:_____
Telephone:_____
E-ail:_____
Congressional District/Senatorial State/ Presidential_____
Date_____

Mail your Tea Party Candidate Pledge to your local Tea Party Group.
Call or e-mail your local Tea Party Organization for an address.

THE REST OF THE STORY

- Abolish the Federal Department of Education
- Enact a Balanced Budget Amendment/a Zero Debt Plan
- Transfer General Welfare and Revenues to the States
- Immigration Reform/Modify the 14th Amendment
- Introduce a Volunteer National Service Plan/with Benefits
- Maintain Funds for National Defense
- Maintain Federal Funds for Natural Disasters
- Establish a Research and Development Fund:
- Promote and Accelerate All forms of Energy
- Establish a Federal Referendum to Limit Taxation
- Create a Commission for Congressional Benefits Reform
- Create a Commission for Congressional Campaign Reform
- Create a Commission for Congressional Protocol Reform
- **Support elected officials only—no czars**

HERE'S SOMETHING WE CAN DO RIGHT NOW TO REDUCE THE NATIONAL DEBT!

More than 500 billion dollars may be saved this fiscal year alone by immediately placing a moratorium on several federal bureaucracies that duplicate state agencies. A permanent removal of the following redundant federal departments, along with Senator Rand Paul's recommendations, would offset a trillion dollars of debt every two years.

Let's start with the following three: The Department of Education, The Department of Energy and The Environmental Protection Agency.

There are more superfluous federal agencies that must be ferreted out. We haven't had a good house cleaning since the Grace Commission back in the early eighties. Duplicating state agencies is extremely wasteful. Let's allow the states to compete among themselves to bring down costs and elevate quality. Fifty states and territories are far more competitive than one monopolistic federal government. Earmarks should be permanently abolished; this wasteful spending would reach the trillion dollar mark, indexed for inflation, within a generation.

We have a morbidly obese federal government. Uncle Sam must consider a financial diet or die. It's past time to rid ourselves of the astronomical financial waste leading us to national bankruptcy. Let's secure the blessings of a balanced budget for every American today and for posterity.

Note: Senator Rand Paul of Kentucky believes we can reduce wasteful spending by eliminating the following: Tens of billions of dollars in spending gone from the departments of education, agriculture, transportation, energy, housing and urban development. Further, he takes on international aid, Health and Human

ACKNOWLEDGEMENTS

Acknowledging the people with whom there was a sharing of strictly American values, including the ethic of hard work, is a matter of gratitude and common courtesy.

Tony Di Marco, a professional writer, motivated me to write "Patriot Papers." He made my fantasy a reality. His encouragement and kindly guidance was instrumental in giving me the confidence to move forward with the book. It helped a great deal to have Tony in my corner. Tony is so modest; his successful writing career would never come from his lips. I have been proud to call Tony a friend and cousin-even before I knew of his many gifts. I thank you Tony from the deepest depths of my heart.

Gratitude and an unmatched love prevail for my wife, Jo. She, fortunately, was my severest and most constructive critic. Jo's tireless daily attention to content and spelling gaffs was very much appreciated. Her sage advice was most welcome and instrumental in the timely completion of the book. Jo, a former teacher, contributed an article of her own, "Financial Reform or Bust". The article can be found in Part 3.

Thank you Jo for your understanding and patience; I don't know if I should thank you or God for being in my life—perhaps, both.

Mitch Terrusa, my beloved son, and indispensable co-worker is a master teacher of computer skills. Mitch's talents were not limited to computer expertise. Mitch's way with words can be observed in the preface of the book, which he wrote. He has contributed efforts in Part 3 of the book, as well. It may have taken me years to complete the project with my limited computer technique. Mitch was another set of eyes looking for writing errors. We enjoyed a similar sense of humor which made the effort less tedious. Thanks again, Mitch.

My other beloved son, David Terrusa, used his computer knowledge to expedite the completion of the project by transmitting several articles to the ultimate editor and publisher. Dave also commented on those articles. I am proud of David's can-do spirit. Thank you, David.

Betsy Betraun, our wonderful friend, was extremely kind and encouraging by giving her most astute opinions of many articles. It is wonderful to have a patriot and a friend who appreciates what is happening in the country and is willing to do whatever is necessary to keep America a great nation. We have adopted Betsy as a member of our family. Thank you, Betsy.

Let's acknowledge the Ventura County Star and the Camarillo Acorn. The editor of the Ventura County Star was extremely helpful in taking the time to discuss, how to keep my articles within their printing standards, Thank you, Mike Craft.

The shared values and diligence has been a family affair with the goal of advancing the greatest country in the world. We, the people, are the recipients of God blessing America and its natural stewards. Eternal vigilance is the price for our God-given inheritance of freedom.

About the Author

Sal Terrusa was born and raised in the Silver Lake district, just north of downtown Los Angeles. He went to UCLA on a football scholarship and served in the Army in Japan during the Korean War. Following his military service and thanks to the G.I. Bill, he earned his master's from California State University-Northridge. He combined a 30-year teaching and coaching career with two successful business ventures, a summer camp for boys and girls and a driving school that had more than 55 employees. After retiring from teaching and business he became a political activist. Sal's children are David, Mitchell, Julie and Leslie. He and wife Jo, when not traveling throughout the U.S., reside in Livingston, Texas.

PATRIOT PAPERS

COVER DESIGNED BY
Mitchell Terrusa

INTERIOR DESIGNED BY
Trans Media Images

LaVergne, TN USA
20 February 2011
217169LV00005B/2/P